THE
PREMIER BOOK
OF
MAJOR POETS

An Anthology

Edited by ANITA DORE

FAWCETT PREMIER • NEW YORK

ACKNOWLEDGMENTS AND COPYRIGHT NOTICES

For permission to use the copyrighted poems included in this volume acknowledgment is made to the following publishers, authors, and agents:

CHARING CROSS MUSIC for selections from "The Sound of Silence" by Paul Simon, © 1964 Charing Cross Music, Inc.

CITY LIGHTS BOOKS for "A Supermarket in California," from *Howl and Other Poems,* copyright © 1956, 1959 by Allen Ginsberg.

COLLINS-KNOWLTON-WING, INC., for "The Portrait" from *Collected Poems,* published by Doubleday & Co., Inc., copyright © 1961 by Robert Graves.

DODD, MEAD & COMPANY for "We Wear the Mask" and "Then and Now" by Paul Laurence Dunbar.

DOUBLEDAY & COMPANY, INC., for "Dolor" by Theodore Roethke, copyright 1934 by Modern Poetry Association, Inc.; for "My Papa's Waltz" by Theodore Roethke, copyright 1942 by Hearst Magazines, Inc.; and for "In a Dark Time" by Theodore Roethke, copyright © 1960 by Beatrice Roethke as Executrix of the Estate of Theodore Roethke, all from *The Collected Poems of Theodore Roethke;* and for "A Small Score," copyright © 1958 by Delmore Schwartz from *Summer Knowledge* by Delmore Schwartz.

(The four pages following constitute an extension of this copyright page.)

CONTENTS

Creatures

Portraits

Stories

Love

Generation

Humor

Places . . . Home and Away

Belief

Commitment

Protest

War

Death

Alienation

Human Condition

20   CONTENTS

Meaning of Life

INTRODUCTION

When a skier glides down a slope with a spray of snow rising behind him—when a surfer roars onto the beach on the crest of a wave—when a fullback breaks from the swarm and runs to daylight—when a child tries his first steps with the awkward grace of uncertainty, we say it is "poetry in motion."

When a novelist writes a scene so vibrant that we live with the excitement of it—when a politician uses words that stir our emotions for years afterwards—when a scientist crystalizes his concepts of space and time, we say it is "sheer poetry."

These are our unconscious tributes to the perfection of poetry.

For perhaps three hundred years, poetry has not had such strong support or so many adherents as it has today. Poetry has accompanied the struggle for civil rights; poetry has heralded man's first steps on the moon, introduced the inauguration of our youngest president, and formed a part of the career of a presidential candidate supported by the youth of this country. Poets and poetry have, in this decade, played an esteemed and prominent role in our nation's pragmatic life.

The reason is clear. The poet is essential.

We look to him in moments of crisis to express our deepest and truest thoughts. For the poet's words and arrangement of words are unique in that they are the essence of thought, a distilled language of ideas.

Because of this process of distillation, it is up to us, the readers, to expand the poet's thoughts, to fill in the gaps, to make the dizzying leap from a symbol to an enormous context of ideas, to understand what is really meant by these suggestive phrases that may at first glance seem disconnected and on second, third, and tenth readings seem to probe to the heart of our most profound and personal emotions.

As our historic perspective of Troy more than three thousand years ago is unalterably influenced by the poet's eye, it is entirely possible that three millenia from today what the citizen knows of the culture, lives, thoughts, and day-to-day emotions of people living in these past few hundred years will be understood to a great extent from the words of the poets in this book.

ANITA DORE

Nature

"In wildness is the preservation of the world."
—HENRY DAVID THOREAU

Voyage to the Moon

Presence among us,

       wanderer in our skies,

dazzle of silver in our leaves and on our
waters silver,

      O
silver evasion in our farthest thought—
"the visiting moon" . . . "the glimpses of the moon" . . .

and we have touched you!

           From the first of time,
before the first of time, before the
first men tasted time, we thought of you.
You were a wonder to us, unattainable,
a longing past the reach of longing,
a light beyond our light, our lives—perhaps
a meaning to us . . .

      Now
our hands have touched you in your depth of night.

Three days and three nights we journeyed,
steered by farthest stars, climbed outward,
crossed the invisible tide-rip where the floating dust
falls one way or the other in the void between,
followed that other down, encountered
cold, faced death—unfathomable emptiness . . .

Then, the fourth day evening, we descended,
made fast, set foot at dawn upon your beaches,
sifted between our fingers your cold sand.

We stand here in the dusk, the cold, the silence . . .

and here, as at the first of time, we lift our heads.
Over us, more beautiful than the moon, a

moon, a wonder to us, unattainable,
a longing past the reach of longing,
a light beyond our light, our lives—perhaps
a meaning to us . . .

O, a meaning!

over us on these silent beaches the bright
earth,
    presence among us.
                    —ARCHIBALD MACLEISH (b. 1892)

With How Sad Steps, O Moon

With how sad steps, O Moon, thou climb'st the skies!
How silently, and with how wan a face!
What, may it be that even in heav'nly place
That busy archer his sharp arrows tries?
Sure, if that long-with-love-acquainted eyes
Can judge of love, thou feel'st a lover's case.
I read it in thy looks; thy languished grace,
To me that feel the like, thy state descries.
Then, ev'n of fellowship, O Moon, tell me,
Is constant love deemed there but want of wit?
Are beauties there as proud as here they be?
Do they above love to be loved, and yet
Those lovers scorn whom that love doth possess?
Do they call virtue there ungratefulness?
                    —SIR PHILIP SIDNEY (1554–1586)

To the Moon

        Art thou pale for weariness
    Of climbing heaven, and gazing on the earth,
        Wandering companionless
    Among the stars that have a different birth,—
And ever-changing, like a joyless eye
That finds no object worth its constancy?
                    —PERCY BYSSHE SHELLEY (1792–1822)

When I Heard the Learned Astronomer

When I heard the learned astronomer,
When the proofs, the figures, were ranged in columns before
    me,
When I was shown the charts and diagrams, to add, divide,
    and measure them,
When I sitting heard the astronomer where he lectured with
    much applause in the lecture-room,
How soon unaccountable I became tired and sick,
Till rising and gliding out I wandered off by myself,
In the mystical moist night-air, and from time to time,
Looked up in perfect silence at the stars.
                —WALT WHITMAN (1819–1892)

Lucifer in Starlight

On a starr'd night Prince Lucifer uprose.
    Tired of his dark dominion swung the fiend
    Above the rolling ball in cloud part screen'd,
Where sinners hugg'd their spectre of repose.
Poor prey to his hot fit of pride were those.
    And now upon his western wing he lean'd,
    Now his huge bulk o'er Afric's sands careen'd,
Now the black planet shadow'd Arctic snows.
Soaring through wider zones that prick'd his scars
    With memory of the old revolt from Awe,
He reach'd a middle height, and at the stars,
Which are the brain of heaven, he look'd, and sank.
Around the ancient track march'd, rank on rank,
    The army of unalterable law.
                —GEORGE MEREDITH (1828–1909)

Unnatural Powers

For fifty thousand years man has been dreaming of powers
Unnatural to him: to fly like the eagles—this groundling!
  —to breathe under the seas, to voyage to the moon,

To launch like the sky-god intolerable thunder-bolts:
   now he has got them.
How little he looks, how desperately scared and excited,
   like a poisonous insect, and no God pities him.
                 —ROBINSON JEFFERS (1887–1962)

A Small Score

Meek, sang the crickets, wheat, meet, creek,
And the birds sang *tutti,* all of them:
      "Bubble, little,
      Whistle, pretty,
      Trickle, whittle,
      Lipping and dripping
      Sipping the well
      Where the fawn dipped
      Before dawn descended
      And darkness surrendered
      To the rising of the sovereign splendor,
      The great bell and ball
      Of supreme abundance and blazing radiance."
Thus, thus, the little birds sang in charming disorder and full
   chorus
To greet gravely, sweetly and most meetly
The blaze of majesty soaring in great oars,
And their twinkling and carolling grew more and more
   sure as they saw the great roar of awe
       arising surely all over the great blue
           bay above them.
              —DELMORE SCHWARTZ (1913–1966)

The Brave Man

     The sun, that brave man,
     Comes through boughs that lie in wait,
     That brave man.

     Green and gloomy eyes
     In dark forms of the grass
     Run away.

The good stars,
Pale helms and spiky spurs,
Run away.

Fears of my bed,
Fears of life and fears of death,
Run away.

That brave man comes up
From below and walks without meditation,
That brave man.

—WALLACE STEVENS (1879–1955)

The World below the Brine

The world below the brine,
Forests at the bottom of the sea, the branches and leaves,
Sea-lettuce, vast lichens, strange flowers and seeds, the thick
    tangle, openings, and pink turf.
Different colors, pale gray and green, purple, white, and
    gold, the play of light through the water,
Dumb swimmers there among the rocks, coral, gluten, grass,
    rushes, and the aliment of the swimmers,
Sluggish existences grazing there suspended, or slowly crawl-
    ing close to the bottom,
The sperm-whale at the surface blowing air and spray, we
    disporting with his flukes,
The leaden-eyed shark, the walrus, the turtle, the hairy sea-
    leopard, and the sting-ray,
Passions there, wars, pursuits, tribes, sight in those ocean-
    depths, breathing that thick-breathing air, as so many do,
The change thence to the sight here, and to the subtle air
    breathed by beings like us who walk this sphere,
The change onward from ours to that of beings who walk
    other spheres.

—WALT WHITMAN (1819–1892)

The Tide Rises, the Tide Falls

The tide rises, the tide falls,
The twilight darkens, the curlew calls;
Along the sea-sands damp and brown
The traveller hastens toward the town,
   And the tide rises, the tide falls.

Darkness settles on roofs and walls,
But the sea, the sea in the darkness calls;
The little waves, with their soft, white hands,
Efface the footprints in the sands,
   And the tide rises, the tide falls.

The morning breaks; the steeds in their stalls
Stamp and neigh, as the hostler calls;
The day returns, but nevermore
Returns the traveller to the shore,
   And the tide rises, the tide falls.
    —HENRY WADSWORTH LONGFELLOW (1807–1882)

Sea Lullaby

The old moon is tarnished
With smoke of the flood,
The dead leaves are varnished
With colour like blood.

A treacherous smiler
With teeth white as milk,
A savage beguiler
In sheathings of silk.

The sea creeps to pillage,
She leaps on her prey;
A child of the village
Was murdered today.

She came up to meet him
In a smooth golden cloak,

She choked him and beat him
To death, for a joke.

Her bright locks were tangled,
She shouted for joy,
With one hand she strangled
A strong little boy.

Now in silence she lingers
Beside him all night
To wash her long fingers
In silvery light.

—ELINOR WYLIE (1885–1928)

I Taste a Liquor Never Brewed

I taste a liquor never brewed,
From tankards scooped in pearl;
Not all the vats upon the Rhine
Yield such an alcohol!

Inebriate of air am I,
And debauchee of dew,
Reeling, through endless summer days,
From inns of molten blue.

When landlords turn the drunken bee
Out of the foxglove's door,
When butterflies renounce their drams,
I shall but drink the more!

Till seraphs swing their snowy hats,
And saints to windows run,
To see the little tippler
Leaning against the sun!

—EMILY DICKINSON (1830–1886)

Cuckoo Song

Sumer is icumen in,
Lhude sing cuccu!
Groweth sed and bloweth med
And springth the wode nu.
Sing cuccu!

Awe bleteth after lomb
Lhouth after calve cu,
Bulluc sterteth, bucke verteth.
Murie sing cuccu!
Cuccu, cuccu,
Wel singes thu, cuccu.
Ne swik thu naver nu!

Sing cuccu nu, Sing cuccu!
Sing cuccu, Sing cuccu nu!
      —Medieval Poem, Author Unknown

Ancient Music

Winter is icumen in,
Lhude sing Goddamm,
Raineth drop and staineth slop,
And how the wind doth ramm!
    Sing : Goddamm.
Skiddeth bus and sloppeth us,
An ague hath my ham.
Freezeth river, turneth liver,
    Damm you, sing : Goddamm.
Goddamm, Goddamm, 'tis why I am, Goddamm,
    So 'gainst the winter's balm.
Sing goddamm, damm, sing Goddamm,
Sing goddamm, sing goddamm, DAMM.
      —Ezra Pound (b. 1885)

Lhude, loud; *med,* meadow; *nu,* now; *awe,* ewe; *lhouth,* lows; *cu,* cow; *sterteth,* leaps up; *verteth,* snorts; *murie,* merry; *swik,* cease.

The Onset

Always the same, when on a fated night
At last the gathered snow lets down as white
As may be in dark woods, and with a song
It shall not make again all winter long
Of hissing on the yet uncovered ground,
I almost stumble looking up and round,
As one who overtaken by the end
Gives up his errand, and lets death descend
Upon him where he is, with nothing done
To evil, no important triumph won,
More than if life had never been begun.

Yet all the precedent is on my side:
I know that winter death has never tried
The earth but it has failed: the snow may heap
In long storms an undrifted four feet deep
As measured against maple, birch and oak,
It cannot check the peeper's silver croak;
And I shall see the snow all go down hill
In water of a slender April rill
That flashes tail through last year's withered brake
And dead weeds, like a disappearing snake.
Nothing will be left white but here a birch,
And there a clump of houses with a church.

—ROBERT FROST (1874–1963)

Written in March

The cock is crowing,
The stream is flowing,
The small birds twitter,
The lake doth glitter,
The green field sleeps in the sun:
The oldest and youngest
Are at work with the strongest:
The cattle are grazing,
Their heads never raising,
There are forty feeding like one!

Like an army defeated,
The snow hath retreated,
And now doth fare ill
On top of the bare hill;
The ploughboy is whooping—anon—anon:
There's joy in the mountains,
There's life in the fountains;
Small clouds are sailing,
Blue sky prevailing,
The rain is over and gone!
                —WILLIAM WORDSWORTH (1770–1850)

Summer

Winter is cold-hearted,
  Spring is yea and nay,
Autumn is a weathercock
    Blown every way.
  Summer days for me
When every leaf is on its tree;

  When Robin's not a beggar,
    And Jenny Wren's a bride,
And larks hang singing, singing, singing
    Over the wheat-fields wide,
    And anchored lilies ride,
    And the pendulum spider
    Swings from side to side;

And blue-black beetles transact business,
    And gnats fly in a host,
And furry caterpillars hasten
    That no time be lost
    And moths grow fat and thrive,
    And ladybirds arrive

  Before green apples blush,
  Before green nuts embrown,
  Why one day in the country
  Is worth a month in town;
  Is worth a day and a year

Of the dusty, musty, lag-last fashion
   That days drone elsewhere.
                              —CHRISTINA ROSSETTI (1830–1894)

These Are the Days When Birds Come Back

These are the days when Birds come back—
A very few—a Bird or two—
To take a backward look.

These are the days when skies resume
The old-old sophistries of June—
A blue and gold mistake.

Oh fraud that cannot cheat the Bee—
Almost thy plausibility
Induces my belief.

Till ranks of seeds their witness bear—
And softly thro' the altered air
Hurries a timid leaf!

Oh Sacrament of summer days,
Oh Last Communion in the Haze—
Permit a child to join.

Thy sacred emblems to partake—
Thy consecrated bread to take
And thine immortal wine!
                              —EMILY DICKINSON (1830–1886)

No!

No sun—no moon!
No morn—no noon—
No dawn—no dusk—no proper time of day—
No sky—no earthly view—
No distance looking blue—
No road—no street—no "t'other side the way"—
No end to any Row—

No indications where the Crescents go—
No top to any steeple—
No recognitions of familiar people—
No courtesies for showing 'em—
No knowing 'em—
No travelling at all—no locomotion,
No inkling of the way—no notion—
"No go"—by land or ocean—
No mail—no post—
No news from any foreign coast—
No Park—no Ring—no afternoon gentility—
No company—no nobility—
No warmth, no cheerfulness, no healthful ease
No comfortable feel in any member—
No shade, no shine, no butterflies, no bees
No fruits, no flowers, no leaves, no birds,
November!

—THOMAS HOOD (1799–1845)

To Autumn

Season of mists and mellow fruitfulness!
  Close bosom-friend of the maturing sun;
Conspiring with him how to load and bless
  With fruit the vines that round the thatch-eaves run;
To bend with apples the moss'd cottage-trees,
  And fill all fruit with ripeness to the core;
    To swell the gourd, and plump the hazel shells
  With a sweet kernel; to set budding more,
And still more, later flowers for the bees,
Until they think warm days will never cease,
  For Summer has o'er-brimm'd their clammy cells.

Who hath not seen thee oft amid thy store?
  Sometimes whoever seeks abroad may find
Thee sitting careless on a granary floor,
  Thy hair soft-lifted by the winnowing wind,
Or on a half-reap'd furrow sound asleep,
  Drowsed with the fume of poppies, while thy hook
    Spares the next swath and all its twinèd flowers;
And sometimes like a gleaner thou dost keep
  Steady thy laden head across a brook;

Or by a cider-press, with patient look,
 Thou watchest the last oozings hours by hours.

Where are the songs of Spring? Ay, where are they?
 Think not of them, thou hast thy music too,—
While barrèd clouds bloom the soft-dying day,
 And touch the stubble-plains with rosy hue;
Then in a wailful choir the small gnats mourn
 Among the river sallows, borne aloft
  Or sinking as the light wind lives or dies;
And full-grown lambs loud bleat from hilly bourn;
 Hedge-crickets sing; and now with treble soft
 The red-breast whistles from a garden-croft;
  And gathering swallows twitter in the skies.
     —JOHN KEATS (1795–1821)

The Sky Is Low, the Clouds Are Mean

The sky is low, the clouds are mean,
A travelling flake of snow
Across a barn or through a rut
Debates if it will go.

A narrow wind complains all day
How some one treated him;
Nature, like us, is sometimes caught
Without her diadem.
     —EMILY DICKINSON (1830–1886)

Ode to the West Wind

I

O wild West Wind, thou breath of Autumn's being,
Thou, from whose unseen presence the leaves dead
Are driven, like ghosts from an enchanter fleeing,

Yellow, and black, and pale, and hectic red,
Pestilence-stricken multitudes: O thou,
Who chariotest to their dark wintry bed

The wingèd seeds, where they lie cold and low,
Each like a corpse within its grave, until
Thine azure sister of the Spring shall blow

Her clarion o'er the dreaming earth, and fill
(Driving sweet buds like flocks to feed in air)
With living hues and odors plain and hill:

Wild Spirit, which art moving everywhere;
Destroyer and preserver; hear, oh, hear!

II

Thou on whose stream, mid the steep sky's commotion,
Loose clouds like earth's decaying leaves are shed,
Shook from the tangled boughs of Heaven and Ocean,

Angels of rain and lightning: there are spread
On the blue surface of thine airy surge,
Like the bright hair uplifted from the head

Of some fierce Maenad,[1] even from the dim verge
Of the horizon to the zenith's height,
The locks of the approaching storm. Thou dirge

Of the dying year, to which this closing night
Will be the dome of a vast sepulcher,
Vaulted with all thy congregated might

Of vapors, from whose solid atmosphere
Black rain, and fire, and hail will burst: oh, hear!

III

Thou who didst waken from his summer dreams
The blue Mediterranean, where he lay,
Lulled by the coil of his crystalline streams,

Beside a pumice isle in Baiae's [2] bay,
And saw in sleep old palaces and towers
Quivering within the wave's intenser day,

[1] *Maenad:* priestess of Bacchus, the god of wine.
[2] *Baiae:* a seaside town at the western end of the Bay of Naples.

All overgrown with azure moss and flowers
So sweet, the sense f ints picturing them! Thou
For whose path the Atlantic's level powers

Cleave themselves into chasms, while far below
The sea-blooms and the oozy woods which wear
The sapless foliage of the ocean, know

Thy voice, and suddenly grow gray with fear,
And tremble and despoil themselves: oh, hear!

IV

If I were a dead leaf thou mightest bear;
If I were a swift cloud to fly with thee;
A wave to pant beneath thy power, and share

The impulse of thy strength, only less free
Than thou, O uncontrollable! If even
I were as in my boyhood, and could be

The comrade of thy wanderings over heaven,
As then, when to outstrip thy skyey speed
Scarce seemed a vision; I would ne'er have striven

As thus with thee in prayer in my sore need.
Oh, lift me as a wave, a leaf, a cloud!
I fall upon the thorns of life! I bleed!

A heavy weight of hours has chained and bowed
One too like thee: tameless, and swift, and proud.

V

Make me thy lyre, even as the forest is:
What if my leaves are f lling like its own!
The tumult of thy mighty harmonies

Will take from both a deep, autumnal tone,
Sweet though in sadness. Be thou, Spirit fierce,
My spirit! Be thou me, impetuous one!

Drive my dead thoughts over the universe
Like withered leaves to quicken a new birth!
And, by the incantation of this verse,

Scatter, as from an unextinguished hearth
Ashes and sparks, my words among mankind!
Be through my lips to unawakened earth

The trumpet of a prophecy! O Wind,
If Winter comes, can Spring be far behind?
                    —PERCY BYSSHE SHELLEY (1792–1822)

The Tree

I stood still and was a tree amid the wood,
Knowing the truth of things unseen before;
Of Daphne [1] and the laurel bough
And that god-feasting couple old
That grew elm-oak amid the wold.
'Twas not until the gods had been
Kindly entreated, and been brought within
Unto the hearth of their heart's home
That they might do this wonder thing;
Nathless I have been a tree amid the wood
And many a new thing understood
That was rank folly to my head before.
                    —EZRA POUND (b. 1885)

Essential Oils Are Wrung

Essential oils are wrung:
The attar from the rose
Is not expressed by suns alone,
It is the gift of screws.

The general rose decays;
But this, in lady's drawer,
Makes summer when the lady lies
In ceaseless rosemary.
                    —EMILY DICKINSON (1830–1886)

[1] *Daphne:* was changed into a laurel tree by the river gods to save her from Apollo's pursuit.

Two Voices in a Meadow

A Milkweed

Anonymous as cherubs
Over the crib of God,
White seeds are floating
Out of my burst pod.
What power had I
Before I learned to yield?
Shatter me, great wind:
I shall possess the field.

A Stone

As casual as cow-dung
Under the crib of God,
I lie where chance would have me,
Up to the ears in sod.
Why should I move? To move
Befits a light desire.
The sill of Heaven would founder,
Did such as I aspire.

—RICHARD WILBUR (b. 1921)

Mushrooms

Overnight, very
Whitely, discreetly,
Very quietly

Our toes, our noses
Take hold on the loam,
Acquire the air.

Nobody sees us,
Stops us, betrays us;
The small grains make room.

Soft fists insist on
Heaving the needles,
The leafy bedding,

Even the paving.
Our hammers, our rams,
Earless and eyeless,

Perfectly voiceless,
Widen the crannies,
Shoulder through holes. We

Diet on water,
On crumbs of shadow,
Bland-mannered, asking

Little or nothing.
So many of us!
So many of us!

We are shelves, we are
Tables, we are meek,
We are edible,

Nudgers and shovers
In spite of ourselves.
Our kind multiplies:

We shall by morning
Inherit the earth.
Our foot's in the door.
                    —SYLVIA PLATH (1932–1963)

Haiku

Red cold
guffaw of summer,
slice
of watermelon!
                    —JOSÉ JUAN TABLADA (1871–1945)
        TRANSLATED BY SAMUEL BECKETT (b. 1906)

Pied Beauty

Glory be to God for dappled things—
   For skies of couple-color as a brinded cow;
     For rose-moles all in stipple upon trout that swim;
Fresh-firecoal chestnut-falls; finches' wings;
   Landscape plotted and pieced—fold, fallow, and plow;
     And áll trádes, their gear and tackle and trim.

All things counter, original, spare, strange;
   Whatever is fickle, freckled (who knows how?)
     With swift, slow; sweet, sour; adazzle, dim;
He fathers-forth whose beauty is past change:
                Praise him.
       —GERARD MANLEY HOPKINS (1844–1889)

Triads

I

The word of the sun to the sky,
   The word of the wind to the sea,
     The word of the moon to the night,
       What may it be?

II

The sense to the flower of the fly,
   The sense of the bird to the tree,
     The sense to the cloud of the light,
       Who can tell me?

III

The song of the fields to the kye,
   The song of the lime to the bee,
     The song of the depth to the height,
       Who knows all three?
  —ALGERNON CHARLES SWINBURNE (1837–1909)

Creatures

"And let man have dominion over the fish of the sea, and over the fowl of the air, and over the cattle . . . and over every creeping thing."
—GENESIS 1:26

A Considerable Speck

A speck that would have been beneath my sight
On any but a paper sheet so white
Set off across what I had written there.
And I had idly poised my pen in air
To stop it with a period of ink
When something strange about it made me think.
This was no dust speck by my breathing blown,
But unmistakably a living mite
With inclinations it could call its own.
It paused as with suspicion of my pen,
And then came racing wildly on again
To where my manuscript was not yet dry;
Then paused again and either drank or smelt—
With loathing, for again it turned to fly.
Plainly with an intelligence I dealt.
It seemed too tiny to have room for feet,
Yet must have had a set of them complete
To express how much it didn't want to die.
It ran with terror and with cunning crept.
It faltered; I could see it hesitate;
Then in the middle of the open sheet
Cower down in desperation to accept
Whatever I accorded it of fate.

I have none of the tenderer-than-thou
Collectivistic regimenting love
With which the modern world is being swept.
But this poor microscopic item now!
Since it was nothing I knew evil of
I let it lie there till I hope it slept.

I have a mind myself and recognize
Mind when I meet with it in any guise.
No one can know how glad I am to find
On any sheet the least display of mind.

—Robert Frost (1874–1963)

47

To a Louse

On Seeing One on a Lady's Bonnet at Church

Ha! whare ye gaun, ye crowlin' ferlie?
Your impudence protects you sairly;
I canna say but ye strunt rarely
      Owre gauze and lace,
Tho' faith! I fear ye dine but sparely
      On sic a place.

Ye ugly, creepin', blastit wonner,
Detested, shunned by saunt an' sinner,
How daur ye set your fit upon her—
      Sae fine a lady!
Gae somewhere else and seek your dinner
      On some poor body.

Swith! in some beggar's hauffet squattle:
There ye may creep and sprawl and sprattle,
Wi' ither kindred, jumping cattle,
      In shoals and nations;
Whare horn nor bane ne'er daur unsettle
      Your thick plantations.

Now haud you there! ye're out o' sight,
Below the fatt'rils, snug an' tight;
Na, faith ye yet! ye'll no be right
      Till ye've got on it—
The vera tapmost, tow'ring height
      O' Miss's bonnet.

My sooth! right bauld ye set your nose out,
As plump an' grey as onie grozet;
O for some rank, mercurial rozet,
      Or fell red smeddum,
I'd gie ye sic a hearty dose o't,
      Wad dress your droddum.

ferlie, wonder; *sairly*, greatly; *strunt*, strut; *fit*, feet; *hauffet*, head; *squattle*, sprawl; *sprattle*, struggle; *bane*, bonecomb; *haud*, stav; *fatt'rils*, ribbon ends; *onie grozet*, any gooseberry; *rozet*, rosin; *fell*, deadly; **smeddum**, powder; **wad . . . droddum**, would put an end to you.

I wad na been surprised to spy
      You on an auld wife's flainen toy;
Or aiblins some bit duddie boy,
        On 's wyliecoat;
    But Miss's fine Lunardi! fye!
        How daur ye do't?

O Jenny, dinna toss your head,
An' set your beauties a' abroad!
Ye little ken what cursèd speed
      The blastie's makin'!
Thae winks an' finger-ends, I dread,
      Are notice takin'!

O wad some Power the giftie gie us
To see oursels as ithers see us!
It wad frae monie a blunder free us,
      An' foolish notion;
What airs in dress an' gait wad lea'e us,
      An' ev'n devotion!
           —ROBERT BURNS (1759–1796)

The Fly

O hideous little bat, the size of snot,
With polyhedral eye and shabby clothes,
To populate the stinking cat you walk
The promontory of the dead man's nose,
Climb with the fine leg of a Duncan Phyfe
      The smoking mountains of my food
        And in a comic mood
In mid-air take to bed a wife.

Riding and riding with your filth of hair
On gluey foot or wing, forever coy,
Hot from the compost and green sweet decay
Sounding your buzzer like an urchin toy;
You dot all whiteness with diminutive stool;

flainen toy, flannel cap; *aiblins,* perhaps; *duddie,* ragged; *wyliecoat,*
flannel vest; *Lunardi,* bonnet; *abroad,* abroad.

In the tight belly of the dead
    Burrow with hungry head
And inlay maggots like a jewel.

At your approach the great horse stomps and paws
Bringing the hurricane of his heavy tail;
Shod in disease you dare to kiss my hand
Which sweeps against you like an angry flail;
Still you return, return, trusting your wing
    To draw you from the hunter's reach
      That learns to kill to teach
    Disorder to the tinier thing.

My peace is your disaster. For your death
Children like spiders cup their pretty hands
And wives resort to chemistry of war.
In fens of sticky paper and quicksands
You glue yourself to death. Where you are stuck
    You struggle hideously and beg;
      You amputate your leg
    Imbedded in the amber muck.

But I, a man, must swat you with my hate,
Slap you across the air and crush your flight,
Must mangle with my shoe and smear your blood,
Expose your little guts pasty and white,
Knock your head sidewise like a drunkard's hat,
    Pin your wings under like a crow's,
      Tear off your flimsy clothes
    And beat you as one beats a rat.

Then like Gargantua I stride among
The corpses strewn like raisins in the dust,
The broken bodies of the narrow dead
That catch the throat with fingers of disgust.
I sweep. One gyrates like a top and falls
    And stunned, stone blind, and deaf
      Buzzes its frightful F
    And dies between three cannibals.

          —KARL SHAPIRO (b. 1913)

To a Skylark

Hail to thee, blithe Spirit!
　　Bird thou never wert,
That from Heaven, or near it,
　　Pourest thy full heart
In profuse strains of unpremeditated art.

Higher still and higher
　　From the earth thou springest
Like a cloud of fire;
　　The blue deep thou wingest,
And singing still dost soar, and soaring ever singest.

In the golden lightning
　　Of the sunken sun,
O'er which clouds are bright'ning,
　　Thou dost float and run;
Like an unbodied joy whose race is just begun.

The pale purple even
　　Melts around thy flight:
Like a star of Heaven,
　　In the broad daylight
Thou art unseen, but yet I hear thy shrill delight,

Keen as are the arrows
　　Of that silver sphere,
Whose intense lamp narrows
　　In the white dawn clear
Until we hardly see—we feel that it is there.

All the earth and air
　　With thy voice is loud,
As, when night is bare,
　　From one lonely cloud
The moon rains out her beams, and Heaven is overflowed.

What thou art we know not;
　　What is most like thee?
From rainbow clouds there flow not
　　Drops so bright to see
As from thy presence showers a rain of melody.

Like a Poet hidden
   In the light of thought,
Singing hymns unbidden,
   Till the world is wrought
To sympathy with hopes and fears it heeded not:

Like a high-born maiden
   In a palace-tower,
Soothing her love-laden
   Soul in secret hour
With music sweet as love, which overflows her bower:

Like a glow-worm golden
   In a dell of dew,
Scattering unbeholden
   Its aërial hue
Among the flowers and grass, which screen it from the view!

Like a rose embowered
   In its own green leaves.
By warm winds deflowered,
   Till the scent it gives
Makes faint with too much sweet those heavy-winged thieves:

Sound of vernal showers
   On the twinkling grass,
Rain-awakened flowers,
   All that ever was
Joyous, and clear, and fresh, thy music doth surpass:

Teach us, Sprite or Bird,
   What sweet thoughts are thine:
I have never heard
   Praise of love or wine
That panted forth a flood of rapture so divine.

Chorus hymeneal,
   Or triumphal chant,
Match'd with thine would be all
   But an empty vaunt—
A thing wherein we feel there is some hidden want.

What objects are the fountains
        Of thy happy strain?
What fields, or waves, or mountains?
        What shapes of sky or plain?
What love of thine own kind? what ignorance of pain?

With thy clear keen joyance
        Languor cannot be:
Shadow of annoyance
        Never came near thee:
Thou lovest; but ne'er knew love's sad satiety.

Waking or asleep
        Thou of death must deem
Things more true and deep
        Than we mortals dream,
Or how could thy notes flow in such a crystal stream?

We look before and after,
        And pine for what is not:
Our sincerest laughter
        With some pain is fraught:
Our sweetest songs are those that tell of saddest thought.

Yet if we could scorn
        Hate, and pride, and fear;
If we were things born
        Not to shed a tear,
I know not how thy joy we ever should come near.

Better than all measures
        Of delightful sound,
Better than all treasures
        That in books are found,
Thy skill to poet were, thou scorner of the ground!

Teach me half the gladness
        That thy brain must know,
Such harmonious madness
        From my lips would flow
The world should listen then, as I am listening now!
                —PERCY BYSSHE SHELLEY (1792–1822)

Lobsters

Here at the Super Duper, in a glass tank
Supplied by a rill of cold fresh water
Running down a glass washboard at one end
And siphoned off at the other, and so
Perpetually renewed, a herd of lobster
Is made available to the customer
Who may choose whichever one he wants
To carry home and drop into boiling water
And serve with a sauce of melted butter.

Meanwhile, the beauty of strangeness marks
These creatures, who move (when they do)
With a slow, vague wavering of claws,
The somnambulist's effortless clambering
As he crawls over the shell of a dream
Resembling himself. Their velvet colors,
Mud red, bruise purple, cadaver green
Speckled with black, their camouflage at home,
Make them conspicuous here in the strong
Day-imitating light, the incommensurable
Philosophers and at the same time victims
Herded together in the marketplace, asleep
Except for certain tentative gestures
Of their antennae, or their imperial claws
Pegged shut with a whittled stick at the wrist.

We inlanders, buying our needful food,
Pause over these slow, gigantic spiders
That spin not. We pause and are bemused,
And sometimes it happens that a mind sinks down
To the blind abyss in a swirl of sand, goes cold
And archaic in a carapace of horn,
Thinking: There's something underneath the world.

The flame beneath the pot that boils the water.
                              —HOWARD NEMEROV (b. 1920)

The Fish

wade
through black jade.
   Of the crow-blue mussel-shells, one keeps
   adjusting the ash-heaps;
      opening and shutting itself like

an
injured fan.
   The barnacles which encrust the side
   of the wave, cannot hide
      there for the submerged shafts of the

sun,
split like spun
   glass, move themselves with spotlight swiftness
   into the crevices—
      in and out, illuminating

the
turquoise sea
   of bodies. The water drives a wedge
   of iron through the iron edge
      of the cliff; whereupon the stars,

pink
rice-grains, ink
   bespattered jelly-fish, crabs like green
   lilies, and submarine
      toadstools, slide each on the other.

All
external
   marks of abuse are present on this
   defiant edifice—
      all the physical features of

ac-
cident—lack
   of cornice, dynamite grooves, burns, and
   hatchet strokes, these things stand
      out on it; the chasm-side is

dead.
Repeated
    evidence has proved that it can live
    on what cannot revive
        its youth. The sea grows old in it.
                    —MARIANNE MOORE (b. 1887)

On a Favorite Cat Drowned in a Tub of Goldfishes

'Twas on a lofty vase's side
Where China's gayest art had dyed
    The azure flowers that blow,
Demurest of the tabby kind,
The pensive Selima, reclined,
    Gazed on the lake below.

Her conscious tail her joy declared:
The fair round face, the snowy beard,
    The velvet of her paws,
Her coat that with the tortoise vies,
Her ears of jet, and emerald eyes,
    She saw, and purr'd applause.

Still had she gazed, but midst the tide
Two angel forms were seen to glide,
    The genii of the stream:
Their scaly armor's Tyrian hue,
Through richest purple, to the view
    Betray'd a golden gleam.

The hapless Nymph with wonder saw:
A whisker first, and then a claw,
    With many an ardent wish,
She stretch'd in vain to reach the prize;
What female heart can gold despise?
    What cat's averse to fish?

Presumptuous maid! with looks intent
Again she stretch'd, again she bent,
    Nor knew the gulf between—

Malignant fate sat by and smiled—
The slippery verge her feet beguiled;
    She tumbled headlong in!

Eight times emerging from the flood
She mew'd to every watery god
    Some speedy aid to send:
No dolphin came, no Nereid stirr'd,
No cruel Tom nor Susan heard—
    A favorite has no friend!
                        —THOMAS GRAY (1716–1771)

A Ritual Mouse

The mouse in the cupboard repeats himself.
Every morning he lies upside down
Astonished at the violence of the spring
That has tumbled him and the flimsy trap again.
His beady expressionless eyes do not speak
Of the terrible moment we sleep through.
Sometimes a little blood runs from his mouth,
Small and dry like his person.
I throw him into the laurel bush as being too small
To give the offenses that occasion burial.

It begins to be winter; he is a field mouse
And comes in, but how unwisely, from the cold.
Elsewhere now, and from their own points of view,
Cats and poisoners are making the same criticism:
He seems no wiser for having been taken
A dozen nights running. He looks weak;
Given a subtler trap he might have informed
Or tried to bargain with whatever it is mice have.

Surely there is always that in experience
Which could warn us; and the worst
That can be said of any of us is:
He did not pay attention.
                        —WILLIAM MEREDITH (b. 1919)

Haiku

The dragon-fly strives patiently
to fasten its transparent cross
to the bare and trembling bough.

*   *   *

Ants on inert cricket crawling.
Memory
of Gulliver in Lilliput.

*   *   *

The tiny monkey looks at me . . .
He would like to tell me something
that escapes his mind!

*   *   *

Although he never stirs from home
the tortoise, like a load of furniture,
jolts down the path.

*   *   *

Lumps of mud, the toads
along the shady path
hop . . .

—JOSÉ JUAN TABLADA (1871–1945)
TRANSLATED BY SAMUEL BECKETT (b. 1906)

A Rabbit Is King of the Ghosts

The difficulty to think at the end of day,
When the shapeless shadow covers the sun
And nothing is left except light on your fur—

There was the cat slopping its milk all day,
Fat cat, red tongue, green mind, white milk
And August the most peaceful month.

To be, in the grass, in the peacefullest time,
Without that monument of cat,
The cat forgotten in the moon;

And to feel that the light is a rabbit-light,
In which everything is meant for you
And nothing need be explained;

Then there is nothing to think of. It comes of itself;
And east rushes west and west rushes down,
No matter. The grass is full

And full of yourself. The trees around are for you,
The whole of the wideness of night is for you,
A self that touches all edges,

You become a self that fills the four corners of night.
The red cat hides away in the fur-light
And there you are humped high, humped up,

You are humped higher and higher, black as stone
You sit with your head like a carving in space
And the little green cat is a bug in the grass.
                              —WALLACE STEVENS (1879–1955)

Snake

A narrow fellow in the grass
Occasionally rides;
You may have met him,—did you not,
His notice sudden is.

The grass divides as with a comb,
A spotted shaft is seen;
And then it closes at your feet
And opens further on.

He likes a boggy acre,
A floor too cool for corn.
Yet when a child, and barefoot,
I more than once, at morn,

Have passed, I thought, a whip-lash
Unbraiding in the sun,—
When, stooping to secure it,
It wrinkled, and was gone.

Several of Natue's people
I know, and they know me;
I feel for them a transport
Of cordiality;

But never met this fellow,
Attended or alone,
Without a tighter breathing,
And zero at the bone.

—EMILY DICKINSON (1830–1886)

The Tiger

Tiger! Tiger! burning bright,
In the forests of the night;
What immortal hand or eye
Could frame thy fearful symmetry?

In what distant deeps or skies
Burnt the fire of thine eyes?
On what wings dare he aspire?
What the hand dare seize the fire?

And what shoulder, and what art,
Could twist the sinews of thy heart?
And when thy heart began to beat,
What dread hand? and what dread feet?

What the hammer? what the chain?
In what furnace was thy brain?
What the anvil? what dread grasp
Dare its deadly terrors clasp?

When the stars threw down their spears,
And watered heaven with their tears,
Did he smile his work to see?
Did he who made the Lamb make thee?

Tiger! Tiger! burning bright,
In the forests of the night;
What immortal hand or eye
Dare frame thy fearful symmetry?

—WILLIAM BLAKE (1757–1827)

Portraits

"*So let us think of people as starting life with an experience they forget, and ending it with one which they anticipate but cannot understand.*"
—E. M. FORSTER

The Giveaway

Saint Bridget was
A problem child.
Although a lass
Demure and mild,
And one who strove
To please her dad,
Saint Bridget drove
The family mad.
For here's the fault in Bridget lay:
She *would* give everything away.

To any soul
Whose luck was out
She'd give her bowl
Of stirabout;
She'd give her shawl,
Divide her purse
With one or all.
And what was worse,
When she ran out of things to give
She'd borrow from a relative.

Her father's gold,
Her grandsire's dinner,
She'd hand to cold
And hungry sinner;
Give wine, give meat,
No matter whose;
Take from her feet
The very shoes,
And when her shoes had gone to others,
Fetch forth her sister's and her mother's.

She could not quit.
She had to share;
Gave bit by bit
The silverware,
The barnyard geese,
The parlor rug,

Her little niece-
'S christening mug,
Even her bed to those in want,
And then the mattress of her aunt.

An easy touch
For poor and lowly,
She gave so much
And grew so holy
That when she died
Of years and fame,
The countryside
Put on her name,
And still the Isles of Erin fidget
With generous girls named Bride or Bridget.

Well, one must love her.
Nonetheless,
In thinking of her
Givingness,
There's no denial
She must have been
A sort of trial
To her kin.
The moral, too, seems rather quaint.
Who had the patience of a saint,
From evidence presented here?
Saint Bridget? Or her near and dear?
　　　　　　　—PHYLLIS MCGINLEY (b. 1905)

She Was a Phantom of Delight

She was a phantom of delight [1]
When first she gleamed upon my sight;
A lovely apparition, sent
To be a moment's ornament;
Her eyes as stars of twilight fair;
Like twilight's, too, her dusky hair;
But all things else about her drawn
From May-time and the cheerful dawn;

[1] Referring to the poet's wife.

A dancing shape, an image gay,
To haunt, to startle, and waylay.

I saw her upon nearer view,
A spirit, yet a woman too!
Her household motions light and free,
And steps of virgin-liberty;
A countenance in which did meet
Sweet records, promises as sweet;
A creature not too bright or good
For human nature's daily food;
For transient sorrows, simple wiles,
Praise, blame, love, kisses, tears, and smiles.

And now I see with eye serene
The very pulse of the machine;
A being breathing thoughtful breath,
A traveller between life and death;
The reason firm, the temperate will,
Endurance, foresight, strength, and skill;
A perfect woman, nobly planned,
To warn, to comfort, and command;
And yet a spirit still, and bright
With something of angelic light.
　　　　　—WILLIAM WORDSWORTH (1770–1850)

Frederick Douglass

When it is finally ours, this freedom, this liberty, this beautiful
and terrible thing, needful to man as air,
usable as earth; when it belongs at last to all,
when it is truly instinct, brain matter, diastole, systole,
reflex action; when it is finally won; when it is more
than the gaudy mumbo jumbo of politicians:
this man, this Douglass, this former slave, this Negro
beaten to his knees, exiled, visioning a world
where none is lonely, none hunted, alien,
this man, superb in love and logic, this man
shall be remembered. Oh, not with statues' rhetoric,
not with legends and poems and wreaths of bronze alone,

but with the lives grown out of his life, the lives
fleshing his dream of the beautiful, needful thing.

—ROBERT HAYDEN (b. 1913)

London, 1802

Milton! thou should'st be living at this hour:
England hath need of thee: she is a fen
Of stagnant waters: altar, sword, and pen,
Fireside, the heroic wealth of hall and bower,
Have forfeited their ancient English dower
Of inward happiness. We are selfish men;
Oh! raise us up, return to us again;
And give us manners, virtue, freedom, power.
Thy soul was like a star, and dwelt apart:
Thou hadst a voice whose sound was like the sea:
Pure as the naked heavens, majestic, free,
So didst thou travel on life's common way,
In cheerful godliness; and yet thy heart
The lowliest duties on herself did lay.

—WILLIAM WORDSWORTH (1770–1850)

To Toussaint L'Ouverture

Toussaint, the most unhappy man of men!
Whether the whistling Rustic tend his plough
Within thy hearing, or thy head be now
Pillowed in some deep dungeon's earless den;—
O miserable Chieftain! where and when
Wilt thou find patience! Yet die not; do thou
Wear rather in thy bonds a cheerful brow:
Though fallen thyself, never to rise again,
Live, and take comfort. Thou hast left behind
Powers that will work for thee; air, earth, and skies;
There's not a breathing of the common wind
That will forget thee; thou hast great allies;
Thy friends are exultations, agonies,
And love, and man's unconquerable mind.

—WILLIAM WORDSWORTH (1770–1850)

O Captain, My Captain!

O Captain! my Captain! our fearful trip is done,[1]
The ship has weather'd every rack, the prize we sought is won.
The port is near, the bells I hear, the people all exulting,
While follow eyes the steady keel, the vessel grim and daring;
    But O heart! heart! heart!
      O the bleeding drops of red,
        Where on the deck my Captain lies,
          Fallen cold and dead.

O Captain! my Captain! rise up and hear the bells;
Rise up—for you the flag is flung—for you the bugle trills,
For you bouquets and ribbon'd wreaths—for you the shores
          a-crowding,
For you they call, the swaying mass, their eager faces turning;
    Here Captain! dear father!
      This arm beneath your head!
        It is some dream that on the deck,
          You've fallen cold and dead.

My Captain does not answer, his lips are pale and still,
My father does not feel my arm, he has no pulse nor will;
The ship is anchor'd safe and sound, its voyage closed and done,
From fearful trip the victor ship comes in with object won;
    Exult O shores, and ring O bells!
      But I with mournful tread,
        Walk the deck my Captain lies,
          Fallen cold and dead.

—WALT WHITMAN (1819–1892)

Ichabod

So fallen! so lost! the light withdrawn
    Which once he wore![2]
The glory from his gray hairs gone
    Forevermore!

[1] Referring to Abraham Lincoln.
[2] Referring to Daniel Webster after his 1850 speech supporting the Missouri Compromise.

Revile him not, the Tempter hath
    A snare for all;
And pitying tears, not scorn and wrath,
    Befit his fall!

Oh, dumb be passion's stormy rage,
    When he who might
Have lighted up and led his age,
    Falls back in night.

Scorn! would the angels laugh, to mark
    A bright soul driven,
Fiend-goaded, down the endless dark,
    From hope and heaven!

Let not the land once proud of him
    Insult him now,
Nor brand with deeper shame his dim,
    Dishonored brow.

But let its humbled sons, instead,
    From sea to lake,
A long lament, as for the dead,
    In sadness make.

Of all we loved and honored, naught
    Save power remains:
A fallen angel's pride of thought,
    Still strong in chains.

All else is gone; from those great eyes
    The soul has fled:
When faith is lost, when honor dies,
    The man is dead!

Then, pay the reverence of old days
    To his dead fame;
Walk backward, with averted gaze,
    And hide the shame!
        —JOHN GREENLEAF WHITTIER (1807–1892)

The Lost Leader

Just for a handful of silver he left us,[1]
    Just for a riband to stick in his coat—
Found the one gift of which fortune bereft us,
    Lost all the others she lets us devote;
They, with the gold to give, doled him out silver,
    So much was theirs who so little allowed:
How all our copper had gone for his service!
    Rags—were they purple, his heart had been proud!
We that had loved him so, followed him, honored him,
    Lived in his mild and magnificent eye,
Learned his great language, caught his clear accents,
    Made him our pattern to live and to die!
Shakespeare was of us, Milton was for us,
    Burns, Shelley, were with us,—they watch from their graves!
He alone breaks from the van and the freemen,
    He alone sinks to the rear and the slaves!

We shall march prospering,—not through his presence;
    Songs may inspirit us,—not from his lyre;
Deeds will be done,—while he boasts his quiescence,
    Still bidding crouch whom the rest bade aspire:
Blot out his name, then, record one lost soul more,
    One task more declined, one more footpath untrod,
One more triumph for devils and sorrow for angels,
    One wrong more to man, one more insult to God!
Life's night begins: let him never come back to us!
    There would be doubt, hesitation and pain,
Forced praise on our part—the glimmer of twilight,
    Never glad confident morning again!
Best fight on well, for we taught him,—strike gallantly,
    Menace our heart ere we master his own;
Then let him receive the new knowledge and wait us,
    Pardoned in Heaven, the first by the throne!
                                    —ROBERT BROWNING (1812–1889)

---

[1] Referring to William Wordsworth in his later conservative years.

A Satirical Elegy on the Death
of a Late Famous General

His Grace! impossible; what, dead! [1]
Of old age too, and in his bed!
And could that mighty warrior fall,
And so inglorious, after all?
Well, since he's gone, no matter how
The last loud trump must wake him now;
And, trust me, as the noise grows stronger,
He'd wish to sleep a little longer.
And could he be indeed so old
As by the newspapers we're told?
Threescore, I think, is pretty high;
'Twas time in conscience he should die!
This world he cumbered long enough;
He burnt his candle to the snuff:
And that's the reason, some folks think,
He left behind so great a stink.
Behold his funeral appears,
Nor widow's sighs, nor orphan's tears,
Wont at such time each heart to pierce,
Attend the progress of his hearse.
But what of that? his friends may say
He had those honors in his day.
True to his profit and his pride,
He made them weep before he died.
    Come hither, all ye empty things!
Ye bubbles raised by breath of kings!
Who float upon the tide of state;
Come hither, and behold your fate!
Let pride be taught by this rebuke,
How very mean a thing's a duke;
From all his ill-got honors flung,
Turned to that dust from whence he sprung.
                    —JONATHAN SWIFT (1667–1745)

---

1 Duke of Marlborough, died June 16, 1722.

Arlo Will

Did you ever see an alligator
Come up to the air from the mud,
Staring blindly under the full glare of noon?
Have you seen the stabled horses at night
Tremble and start back at the sight of a lantern?
Have you ever walked in darkness
When an unknown door was open before you
And you stood, it seemed, in the light of a thousand candles
Of delicate wax?
Have you walked with the wind in your ears
And the sunlight about you,
And found it suddenly shine with an inner splendor?
Out of the mud many times,
Before many doors of light,
Through many fields of splendor,
Where around your steps a soundless glory scatters
Like new-fallen snow,
Will you go through earth, O strong of soul,
And through unnumbered heavens
To the final flame!

—EDGAR LEE MASTERS (1868–1950)

My Last Duchess

That's my last Duchess painted on the wall,
Looking as if she were alive. I call
That piece a wonder, now: Frà Pandolf's hands
Worked busily a day, and there she stands.
Will 't please you sit and look at her? I said
"Frà Pandolf" by design, for never read
Strangers like you that pictured countenance,
The depth and passion of its earnest glance,
But to myself they turned (since none puts by
The curtain I have drawn for you, but I)
And seemed as they would ask me, if they durst
How such a glance came there; so, not the first
Are you to turn and ask thus. Sir, 't was not
Her husband's presence only, called that spot

Of joy into the Duchess' cheek: perhaps
Frà Pandolf chanced to say, "Her mantle laps
Over my lady's wrist too much," or "Paint
Must never hope to reproduce the faint
Half-flush that dies along her throat:" such stuff
Was courtesy, she thought, and cause enough
For calling up that spot of joy. She had
A heart—how shall I say?—too soon made glad.
Too easily impressed: she liked whate'er
She looked on, and her looks went everywhere.
Sir, 't was all one! My favor at her breast,
The dropping of the daylight in the West,
The bough of cherries some officious fool
Broke in the orchard for her, the white mule
She rode with round the terrace—all and each
Would draw from her alike the approving speech,
Or blush, at least. She thanked men—good! but thanked
Somehow—I know not how—as if she ranked
My gift of a nine-hundred-years-old name
With anybody's gift. Who'd stoop to blame
This sort of trifling? Even had you skill
In speech—(which I have not)—to make your will
Quite clear to such an one, and say, "Just this
Or that in you disgusts me; here you miss,
Or there exceed the mark"—and if she let
Herself be lessoned so, nor plainly set
Her wits to yours, forsooth, and made excuse,
Even then would be some stooping; and I choose
Never to stoop. Oh sir, she smiled, no doubt,
Whenever I passed her; but who passed without
Much the same smile? This grew; I gave commands;
Then all smiles stopped together. There she stands
As if alive. Will 't please you rise? We'll meet
The company below, then. I repeat,
The Count your master's known munificence
Is ample warrant that no just pretence
Of mine for dowry will be disallowed:
Though his fair daughter's self, as I avowed
At starting, is my object. Nay, we'll go
Together down, sir. Notice Neptune, though,
Taming a sea-horse, thought a rarity,
Which Claus of Innsbruck cast in bronze for me!

—ROBERT BROWNING (1812–1889)

She Walks in Beauty

She walks in beauty, like the night [1]
 Of cloudless climes and starry skies;
And all that's best of dark and bright
 Meet in her aspect and her eyes:
Thus mellowed to that tender light
 Which heaven to gaudy day denies.

One shade the more, one ray the less,
 Had half impaired the nameless grace
Which waves in every raven tress,
 Or softly lightens o'er her face;
Where thoughts serenely sweet express
 How pure, how dear their dwelling-place.

And on that cheek, and o'er that brow,
 So soft, so calm, yet eloquent,
The smiles that win, the tints that glow,
 But tell of days in goodness spent,
A mind at peace with all below,
 · A heart whose love is innocent!
  —GEORGE GORDON BYRON, LORD BYRON (1788–1824)

The Portrait

She speaks always in her own voice
Even to strangers; but those other women
Exercise their borrowed, or false, voices
Even on sons and daughters.

She can walk invisibly at noon
Along the high road; but those other women
Gleam phosphorescent—broad hips and gross fingers—
Down every lampless alley.

She is wild and innocent, pledged to love
Through all disaster; but those other women

[1] Referring to Byron's cousin, Lady Wilmot Horton.

Decry her for a witch or a common drab
And glare back when she greets them.

Here is her portrait, gazing sidelong at me,
The hair in disarray, the young eyes pleading:
"And you, love? As unlike those other men
As I those other women?"

—ROBERT GRAVES (b. 1895)

Lucinda Matlock

I went to the dances at Chandlerville,
And played snap-out at Winchester.
One time we changed partners,
Driving home in the moonlight of middle June,
And then I found Davis.
We were married and lived together for seventy years,
Enjoying, working, raising the twelve children,
Eight of whom we lost
Ere I had reached the age of sixty.
I spun, wove, kept the house, nursed the sick,
I made the garden, and for holiday
Rambled over the fields where sang the larks,
And by Spoon River gathering many a shell,
And many a flower and medicinal weed—
Shouting to the wooded hills, singing to the green valleys.
At ninety-six I had lived enough, that is all,
And passed a sweet repose.
What is this I hear of sorrow and weariness,
Anger, discontent and drooping hopes?
Degenerate sons and daughters,
Life is too strong for you—
It takes life to love Life.

—EDGAR LEE MASTERS (1868–1950)

She Dwelt among the Untrodden Ways

She dwelt among the untrodden ways
   Beside the springs of Dove,[1]

1 *Dove:* river in England much celebrated by artists and poets.

A maid whom there were none to praise
  And very few to love:

A violet by a mossy stone
  Half hidden from the eye!
—Fair as a star, when only one
  Is shining in the sky.

She lived unknown, and few could know
  When Lucy ceased to be;
But she is in her grave, and, oh,
  The difference to me!
          —WILLIAM WORDSWORTH (1770–1850)

To Helen

Helen, thy beauty is to me
  Like those Nicéan barks of yore,
That gently, o'er a perfumed sea,
  The weary, way-worn wanderer bore
  To his own native shore.

On desperate seas long wont to roam,
  Thy hyacinth hair, thy classic face,
Thy Naiad airs have brought me home
  To the glory that was Greece,
And the grandeur that was Rome.

Lo! in yon brilliant window-niche
  How statue-like I see thee stand,
  The agate lamp within thy hand!
Ah, Psyche, from the regions which
  Are Holy Land!
          —EDGAR ALLAN POE (1809–1849)

Stories

Scheherazade heard the cock crow and knew that it was morning and stopped speaking. And the Sultan, eager to hear the end of the story, spared her life for yet another day.
—Arabian Nights

The Twa Corbies

As I was walking all alane,
I heard twa corbies making a mane,
The tane unto the t'other did say,
"Where sall we gang and dine today?"

"O down beside yon auld fail dyke,
I wot there lies a new-slain knight;
And naebody kens that he lies there,
But his hawk, his hound, and lady fair.

"His hound is to the hunting gane,
His hawk to fetch the wild-fowl hame,
His lady's ta'en another mate,
So we may mak our dinner sweet.

"Ye'll sit on his white hause-bane,
And I'll pike out his bonny blue een;
Wi' ae lock o' his gowden hair
We'll theek our nest when it grows bare.

"Mony a ane for him makes mane,
But nane sall ken where he is gane;
O'er his white banes, when they are bare,
The wind sall blaw for evermair."
　　　　　　—MEDIEVAL POEM, AUTHOR UNKNOWN

The Twin Brothers

There were twa brethren in the North,
　　They went to school thegither;
The one unto the other said,
　　"Will you try a warsle, brither?"

They warsled up, they warsled down,
　　Till Sir John fell to the ground,

corbies, ravens; *mane*, moan; *tane*, one; *sall*, shall; *gang*, go; *dyke*, turf wall; *wot*, know; *kens*, knows; *hause-bane*, neck-bone; *pike*, pick; *een*, eyes; *gowden*, golden; *theek*, thatch; *banes*, bones; *warsle*, wrestle.

And there was a knife in Sir Willie's pouch
    Gied him a deadly wound.

Tak' aff, tak' aff my holland sark,
    Rive it frae gare to gare.
And stap it in my bleeding wound—
    Twill aiblins bleed nae mair?

He's pu'it aff his holland sark,
    Rave it frae gare to gare,
And stapt it in his bleeding wound
    But aye it bled the mair.

O tak' now aff my green cleiding
    And row me saftly in,
And carry me up to Chester kirk.
    Whar the grass grows fair and green.

But what will ye say to your father dear
    When ye gae home at e'en?—
I'll say ye're lying at Chester kirk,
    Whar the grass grows fair and green.—

O no, O no, when he speers for me
    Saying, "William, whar is John?"
Ye'll say ye left me at Chester school
    Leaving the school alone.

He's ta'en him up upo' his back,
    And borne him hence away.
And carried him to Chester kirk
    And laid him in the clay.

But when he sat in his father's chair.
    He grew baith pale and wan:
"O what blude's that upon your brow?
    And whar is your brither John?"—

"O John's awa' to Chester school,
    A scholar he'll return;
He bade me tell his father dear
    About him no' to mourn.

aiblins, perhaps; *cleiding*, clothing; *speers*, asks.

"And it is the blude o' my gude grey steed;
   He wadna hunt for me."—
"O thy steed's blude was ne'er so red,
   Nor ne'er so dear to me!"

"And whaten blude's that upon your dirk?
   Dear Willie, tell to me."—
"It is the blude o' my ae brither
   And dule and wae is me!"—

"O what sall I say to your mither?
   Dear Willie, tell to me."—
"I'll saddle my steed and awa' I'll ride,
   To dwell in some far countrie."—

"O when will ye come hame again?
   Dear Willie, tell to me!"—
"When the sun and moon dance on yon green:
   And that will never be!"

            —OLD BALLAD, AUTHOR UNKNOWN

The Riddling Knight

There were three sisters fair and bright,
   Jennifer, Gentle, and Rosemary,
And they three loved one valiant knight—
   As the dove flies over the mulberry-tree.

The eldest sister let him in
and barr'd the door with a silver pin.

The second sister made his bed,
and placed soft pillows under his head.

The youngest sister that same night
Was resolved for to wed wi' this valiant knight.

"And if you can answer questions three,
O then, fair maid, I'll marry wi' thee.

"O what is louder nor a horn,
Or what is sharper nor a thorn?

"Or what is heavier nor the lead,
  Or what is better nor the bread?

"Or what is longer nor the way,
  Or what is deeper nor the sea?"

"O shame is louder nor a horn,
  And hunger is sharper nor a thorn.

"O sin is heavier nor the lead,
  The blessing's better nor the bread.

"O the wind is longer nor the way
  And love is deeper nor the sea."

You have answer'd aright my questions three,
  Jennifer, Gentle, and Rosemary;
And now, fair maid, I'll marry wi' thee
  As the dove flies over the mulberry-tree.
          —OLD BALLAD, AUTHOR UNKNOWN

The Bayliff's Daughter of Islington

There was a youth, and a well beloved youth,
  And he was a esquire's son,
He loved the bayliff's daughter dear,
  That lived in Islington.

She was coy, and she would not believe
  That he did love her so,
No, nor at any time she would
  Any countenance to him show.

But when his friends did understand
  His fond and foolish mind,
They sent him up to fair London,
  An apprentice for to bind.

And when he had been seven long years,
  And his love he had not seen,

"Many a tear have I shed for her sake
     When she little thought of me."

All the maids of Islington
     Went forth to sport and play—
All but the bayliff's daughter dear—
     She secretly stole away.

She put off her gown of gray,
     And put on her puggish attire
She's up to fair London gone,
     Her true-love to require.

As she went along the road,
     The weather being hot and dry,
There was she aware of her true-love,
     At length came riding by.

She stept to him, as red as any rose,
     And took him by the bridle-ring:
"I pray you, kind sir, give me one penny,
     To ease my weary limb."

"I prithee, sweetheart, canst thou tell me
     Where that thou wast born?"
"At Islington, kind sir," said she,
     "Where I have had many a scorn."

"I prithee, sweetheart, canst thou tell me
     Whether thou dost know
The bayliff's daughter of Islington?"
     "She's dead, sir, long ago."

"Then will I sell my goodly steed,
     My saddle and my bow;
I will into some far country,
     Where no man doth me know."

"O stay, O stay, thou goodly youth;
     She's alive, she is not dead;
Here she standeth by thy side,
     And ready to be thy bride."

"O farewell grief, and welcome joy,
     Ten thousand times and more.

For now I have seen my own true-love,
    That I thought I should have seen no more."
                —OLD BALLAD, AUTHOR UNKNOWN

Get Up and Bar the Door

It fell about the Martinmas time,
    And a gay time it was then,
When our goodwife got puddings to make,
    And she's boiled them in the pan.

The wind so cold blew south and north,
    And blew into the floor;
Quoth our goodman to our goodwife,
    "Get up and bar the door."

"My hand is in my household work,
    Goodman, as ye may see;
And it will not be barred for a hundred years,
    If it's to be barred by me!"

They made a pact between them both,
    They made it firm and sure,
That whosoe'er should speak the first,
    Should rise and bar the door.

Then by there came two gentlemen,
    At twelve o'clock at night,
And they could see neither house nor hall,
    Nor coal nor candlelight.

"Now whether is this a rich man's house,
    Or whether it is a poor?"
But never a word would one of them speak,
    For barring of the door.

The guests they ate the white puddings,
    And then they ate the black;
Tho' much the goodwife thought to herself,
    Yet never a word she spake.

Then said one stranger to the other,
    "Here, man, take ye my knife;

Do ye take off the old man's beard,
   And I'll kiss the goodwife."

"There's no hot water to scrape it off,
   And what shall we do then?"
"Then why not use the pudding broth,
   That boils into the pan?"

O up then started our goodman,
   An angry man was he;
"Will ye kiss my wife before my eyes!
    And with pudding broth scald me!"

Then up and started our goodwife,
   Gave three skips on the floor:
"Goodman, you've spoken the foremost word.
   Get up and bar the door!"
           —OLD BALLAD, AUTHOR UNKNOWN

The Demon Lover

"Oh, where have you been, my long, long love,
   This long seven years and more?"
"Oh, I've come to seek my former vows
   Ye granted me before."

"Oh, do not speak of your former vows,
   For they will breed sad strife;
Oh, do not speak of your former vows,
   For I have become a wife."

He turned him right and round about,
   And the tear blinded his ee:
"I would never have trodden on this ground
   If it had not been for thee."

"If I was to leave my husband dear,
   And my two babes also,
Oh, what have you to take me to,
   If with you I should go?"

"I have seven ships upon the sea—
   The eighth brought me to land—

With four-and-twenty bold mariners,
    And music on every hand."

She has taken up her two little babes,
    Kissed them on cheek and chin:
"Oh, fare ye well, my own two babes,
    For I'll never see you again."

She set her foot upon the ship—
    No mariners could she behold;
But the sails were of the taffeta,
    And the masts of the beaten gold.

She had not sailed a league, a league,
    A league but barely three,
When dismal grew his countenance,
    And drumlie grew his ee.

They had not sailed a league, a league,
    A league but barely three,
Until she espied his cloven foot,
    And she wept right bitterly.

"Oh, hold your tongue of your weeping," said he,
    "Of your weeping now let me be;
I will show you how the lilies grow
    On the banks of Italy."

"Oh, what hills are yon, yon pleasant hills,
    That the sun shines sweetly on?"
"Oh, yon are the hills of heaven," he said,
    "Where you will never win."

"Oh, whaten a mountain is yon," she said,
    "So dreary with frost and snow?"
"Oh, yon is the mountain of hell," he cried,
    "Where you and I will go."

He struck the top-mast with his hand,
    The fore-mast with his knee;
And he broke that gallant ship in twain,
    And sank her in the sea.

                        —OLD BALLAD, AUTHOR UNKNOWN

drumlie: dark.

May Colvin

False Sir John a-wooing came,
  To a maid of beauty rare;
May Colvin was the lady's name,
  Her father's only heir.

He wooed her indoors, he wooed her out,
  He wooed her night and day;
Until he got the lady's consent
  To mount and ride away.

"Go fetch me some of your father's gold
  And some of your mother's fee,
And I'll carry you to the far Northland
  And there I'll marry thee."

She's gone to her father's coffers,
  Where all his money lay;
And she's taken the red, and she's left the white,
  And lightly she's tripped away.

She's gone down to her father's stable,
  Where all his steeds did stand;
And she's taken the best and left the worst,
  That was in her father's land.

He rode on, and she rode on,
  They rode a long summer's day,
Until they came to a broad river,
  An arm of a lonesome sea.

"Leap off the steed," says false Sir John;
  "Your bridal bed you see;
For it's seven fair maids I have drownèd here,
  And the eighth one you shall be.

"Cast off, cast off your silks so fine,
  And lay them on a stone,
For they are too fine and costly
  To rot in the salt sea foam."

"O turn about, thou false Sir John,
　And look to the leaf o' the tree;
For it never became a gentleman
　A naked woman to see."

He's turned himself straight round about
　To look to the leaf o' the tree,
She's twined her arms about his waist,
　And thrown him into the sea.

"O hold a grip of me, May Colvin,
　For fear that I should drown;
I'll take you home to your father's gates,
　And safe I'll set you down."

"O safe enough I am, Sir John,
　And safer I will be;
For seven fair maids have you drownèd here,
　The eighth shall not be me.

"O lie you there, thou false Sir John,
　O lie you there," said she,
"For you lie not in a colder bed
　Then the one you intended for me."

So she went on her father's steed,
　As swift as she could away;
And she came home to her father's gates
　At the breaking of the day.

Up then spake the pretty parrot:
　"May Colvin, where have you been?
What has become of false Sir John,
　That wooed you yestere'en?"

"O hold your tongue, my pretty parrot,
　Nor tell no tales on me;
Your cage will be made of the beaten gold
　With spokes of ivory."

Up then spake her father dear,
　In the chamber where he lay:
"What ails you, pretty parrot,
　That you prattle so long ere day?"

"There came a cat to my door, master,
    I thought 'twould have worried me;
And I was calling on May Colvin
    To take the cat from me."
                    —OLD BALLAD, AUTHOR UNKNOWN

La Belle Dame sans Merci

"Oh, what can ail thee, knight-at-arms,
    Alone and palely loitering?
The sedge has withered from the lake,
    And no birds sing.

"Oh, what can ail thee, knight-at-arms,
    So haggard and so woebegone?
The squirrel's granary is full,
    And the harvest's done.

"I see a lily on thy brow,
    With anguish moist and fever dew;
And on thy cheeks a fading rose
    Fast withereth, too."

I met a lady in the meads,
    Full beautiful—a faëry's child;
Her hair was long, her foot was light,
    And her eyes were wild.

I made a garland for her head,
    And bracelets too, and fragrant zone;
She looked at me as she did love,
    And made sweet moan.

I set her on my pacing steed,
    And nothing else saw, all day long.
For sidelong would she bend, and sing
    A faëry's song.

She found me roots of relish sweet,
    And honey wild, and manna dew;
And sure in language strange she said,
    "I love thee true."

She took me to her elfin grot,
    And there she wept, and sighed full sore;
And there I shut her wild, wild eyes
    With kisses four.

And there she lullèd me asleep,
    And there I dreamed, ah, woe betide!
The latest dream I ever dreamt
    On the cold hill side.

I saw pale kings, and princes, too,
    Pale warriors, death-pale were they all;
They cried, "La Belle Dame Sans Merci
    Hath thee in thrall!"

I saw their starved lips in the gloam
    With horrid warning gapèd wide—
And I awoke, and found me here,
    On the cold hill's side.

And this is why I sojourn here,
    Alone and palely loitering,
Though the sedge is withered from the lake
    And no birds sing.
                        —JOHN KEATS (1795–1821)

Lady Clare

It was the time when lilies blow,
    And clouds are highest up in air,
Lord Ronald brought a lily-white doe
    To give his cousin, Lady Clare.

I trow they did not part in scorn:
    Lovers long-betrothed were they:
They two will wed the morrow morn,—
    God's blessing on the day!

"He does not love me for my birth,
    Nor for my lands so broad and fair;
He loves me for my own true worth,
    And that is well," said Lady Clare.

In there came old Alice the nurse,
    Said, "Who was this that went from thee?"
"It was my cousin," said Lady Clare,
    "To-morrow he weds with me."

"O God be thanked!" said Alice the nurse,
    "That all comes round so just and fair:
Lord Ronald is heir of all your lands,
    And you are *not* the Lady Clare."

"Are ye out of your mind, my nurse, my nurse,"
    Said Lady Clare, "that ye speak so wild?"
"As God's above," said Alice the nurse,
    "I speak the truth: you are my child.

"The old earl's daughter died at my breast;
    I speak the truth, as I live by bread!
I buried her like my own sweet child,
    And put my child in her stead."

"Falsely, falsely have ye done,
    O mother," she said, "if this be true,
To keep the best man under the sun
    So many years from his due."

"Nay now, my child," said Alice the nurse,
    "But keep the secret for your life,
And all you have will be Lord Ronald's,
    When you are man and wife."

"If I'm a beggar born," she said,
    "I will speak out, for I dare not lie.
Pull off, pull off, the brooch of gold,
    And fling the diamond necklace by."

"Nay now, my child," said Alice the nurse,
    "But keep the secret all you can."
She said, "Not so: but I will know
    If there be any faith in man."

"Nay now, what faith?" said Alice the nurse,
    "The man will cleave unto his right."
"And he shall have it," the lady replied,
    "Though I should die to-night."

"Yet give one kiss to your mother dear,
   Alas, my child, I sinned for thee."
"O mother, mother, mother," she said,
   "So strange it seems to me.

"Yet here's a kiss for my mother dear,
   My mother dear, if this be so,
And lay your hand upon my head,
   And bless me, mother, ere I go."

She clad herself in a russet gown,
   She was no longer Lady Clare:
She went by dale, and she went by down,
   With a single rose in her hair.

The lily-white doe Lord Ronald had brought
   Leaped up from where she lay,
Dropped her head in the maiden's hand,
   And followed her all the way.

Down stepped Lord Ronald from his tower:
   "O Lady Clare, you shame your worth!
Why come you dressed like a village maid,
   That are the flower of the earth?"

"If I come dressed like a village maid,
   I am but as my fortunes are:
I am a beggar born," she said,
   "And not the Lady Clare."

"Play me no tricks," said Lord Ronald,
   "For I am yours in word and in deed;
Play me no tricks," said Lord Ronald,
   "Your riddle is hard to read."

O, and proudly stood she up!
   Her heart within her did not fail;
She looked into Lord Ronald's eyes,
   And told him all her nurse's tale.

He laughed a laugh of merry scorn:
   He turned and kissed her where she stood:
"If you are not the heiress born,
   And I," said he, "the next in blood—

"If you are not the heiress born,
    And I," said he, "the lawful heir,
We two will wed to-morrow morn,
    And you shall still be Lady Clare."
        —ALFRED, LORD TENNYSON (1809–1892)

Mandalay

By the old Moulmein Pagoda, lookin' lazy at the sea,
There's a Burma girl a-settin', and I know she thinks o' me;
For the wind is in the palm-trees, and the temple-bells they
    say:
"Come you back, you British soldier; come you back to Man-
    dalay!"
        Come you back to Mandalay,
        Where the old Flotilla lay:
        Can't you 'ear their paddles chunkin' from Rangoon to
            Mandalay?
        On the road to Mandalay,
        Where the flyin'-fishes play,
        An' the dawn comes up like thunder outer China 'crost
            the Bay!

'Er petticoat was yaller an' 'er little cap was green,
An' 'er name was Supi-yaw-lat—jes' the same as Theebaw's
    Queen,
An' I seed her first a-smokin' of a whackin' white cheroot,
An' a-wastin' Christian kisses on an 'eathen idol's foot:
        Bloomin' idol made o' mud—
        Wot they called the Great Gawd Budd—
        Plucky lot she cared for idols when I kissed 'er where
            she stud!
        On the road to Mandalay . . .

When the mist was on the rice-fields an 'the sun was droppin'
    slow,
She'd git 'er little banjo an' she'd sing "*Kulla-lo-lo!*"
With 'er arm upon my shoulder an' 'er cheek agin my cheek
We useter watch the steamers an' the *hathis* pilin' teak.
        Elephints a'pilin' teak.
        In the sludgy, squdgy creek,

> Where the silence 'ung that 'eavy you was 'arf afraid to
>   speak!
> On the road to Mandalay . . .

But that's all shove be'ind me—long ago an' fur away,
An' there ain't no 'busses runnin' from the Bank to Mandalay;
An' I'm learnin' 'ere in London what the ten-year soldier tells:
"If you've 'eard the East a'callin', you won't never 'eed naught
    else."
> No! you won't 'eed nothin' else
> But them spicy garlic smells,
An' the sunshine an' the palm-trees an' the tinkly-temple-
    bells;
> On the road to Mandalay . . .

I am sick o' wastin' leather on these gritty pavin'-stones,
An' the blasted English drizzle wakes the fever in my bones;
Tho' I walks with fifty 'ousemaids outer Chelsea to the
    Strand,
An' they talks a lot o' lovin', but wot do they understand?
> Beefy face an' grubby 'and—
> Law! wot do they understand?
I've a neater, sweeter maiden in a cleaner, greener land!
> On the road to Mandalay . . .

Ship me somewheres east of Suez, where the best is like the
    worst
Where there aren't no Ten Commandments an' a man can
    raise a thirst:
For the temple-bells are callin', an' it's there that I would be—
By the old Moulmein Pagoda, looking lazy at the sea;
> On the road to Mandalay,
> Where the old Flotilla lay,
> With our sick beneath the awnings when we went to
>   Mandalay!
> O the road to Mandalay,
> Where the flyin'-fishes play,
> An' the dawn comes up like thunder outer China 'crost
>   the Bay!

—RUDYARD KIPLING (1865–1936)

Sir Patrick Spens

The king sits in Dunfermling town
  Drinking the blude-red wine;
"O where will I get a gude skipper
  To sail this ship o' mine?"

O up and spake an eldern knight,
  Sat at the king's right knee:
"Sir Patrick Spens is the best sailor
  That ever sail'd the sea."

Our king has written a letter,
  And seal'd it with his hand,
And sent it to Sir Patrick Spens,
  Was walking on the strand.

"To Noroway, to Noroway,
  To Noroway o'er the faem;
The king's daughter o' Noroway,
  'Tis thou must bring her hame."

The first word that Sir Patrick read,
  A loud laugh laughèd he;
The next word that Sir Patrick read,
  The tear blinded his e'e.

"O who is this has done this deed
  This ill deed unto me,
To send us out, at this time o' year,
  To sail upon the sea?

"Be it wind, be it weet, be it hail, be it sleet,
  Our ship must sail the faem;
The king's daughter o' Noroway,
  'Tis we must fetch her hame.

"Make haste, make haste, my merry men all;
  Our gude ship sails the morn."—
"Now ever alack, my master dear,
  I fear a deadly storm.

"Late, late yestreen I saw the new moone
   Wi' the auld moone in her arm;
And I fear, I fear, my master dear,
   That we will come to harm."

They hadna sail'd a league, a league,
   A league but barely three,
When the sky grew dark, and the wind blew loud,
   And angry grew the sea.

The anchors broke, the topmast split,
   It was sic a deadly storm:
And the waves came owre the broken ship
   Till a' her sides were torn.

O loath, loath, were our gude Scots lords
   To wet their cork-heel'd shoon:
But lang or a' the play was play'd
   Their hats they swam aboon.

O lang, lang may the ladies sit,
   Wi' their fans into their hand,
Before they see Sir Patrick Spens
   Come sailing to the strand.

And lang, lang may the maidens sit
   Wi' their gold kames in their hair,
A-waiting for their ain dear loves,
   For them they'll see nae mair.

Half-owre, half-owre to Aberdour,
   'Tis fifty fathoms deep;
And there lies gude Sir Patrick Spens,
   Wi' the Scots lords at his feet.

            —OLD BALLAD, AUTHOR UNKNOWN

The Golden Vanity

There was a gallant ship, a gallant ship was she,
And the name of the ship was "The Golden Vanity,"

aboon, above.

And they feared she would be taken by the Turkish enemy
   As she sailed upon the Lowland, Lowland, Lowland,
   As she sailed upon the Lowland sea.

Then up came a little cabin boy, and thus spoke he,
Speaking to the captain, "What will you give to me
If I swim alongside of the Turkish enemy
   And sink her in the Lowland, Lowland, Lowland,
   And sink her in the Lowland Sea?"

"I'll give you an estate in the North Countrie,
And my one and only daughter your lovely bride shall be,
If you'll swim alongside of the Turkish enemy
   And sink her in the Lowland, Lowland, Lowland,
   And sink her in the Lowland sea."

Then the boy made ready and overboard sprang he,
And swam alongside of the Turkish enemy,
And with his auger sharp in her side he bored holes three,
   And he sunk her in the Lowland, Lowland, Lowland,
   He sunk her in the Lowland sea.

Then the boy swam around, and back again swam he,
And he called to the captain of "The Golden Vanity."
But the captain mocked, "You can drown for all of me!"
   And he left him in the Lowland, Lowland, Lowland,
   He left him in the Lowland sea.

The boy swam around, he came to the port side,
He looked up at his messmates, and bitterly he cried:
"Oh, messmates, take me up, for I'm drifting with the tide,
   And I'm sinking in the Lowland, Lowland, Lowland,
   I'm sinking in the Lowland sea."

His messmates took him up, but on the deck he died,
And they sewed him in a hammock that was so large and wide.
They lowered him overboard, but he drifted with the tide,
   And he sank beneath the Lowland, Lowland, Lowland,
   He sank beneath the Lowland sea.

              —OLD BALLAD, AUTHOR UNKNOWN

The Convergence of the Twain
(*Lines on the loss of the* Titanic)

I.
In a solitude of the sea
Deep from human vanity,
And the Pride of Life that planned her, stilly couches she.

II.
Steel chambers, late the pyres
Of her salamandrine fires,
Cold currents thrid, and turn to rhythmic tidal lyres.

III.
Over the mirrors meant
To glass the opulent
The sea-worm crawls—grotesque, slimed, dumb, indifferent.

IV.
Jewels in joy designed
To ravish the sensuous mind
Lie lightless, all their sparkles bleared and black and blind.

V.
Dim moon-eyed fishes near
Gaze at the gilded gear
And query: "What does this vaingloriousness down here?" . . .

VI.
Well: while was fashioning
This creature of cleaving wing,
The Immanent Will that stirs and urges everything

VII.
Prepared a sinister mate
For her—so gaily great—
A Shape of Ice, for the time far and dissociate.

VIII.
And as the smart ship grew
In stature, grace, and hue,
In shadowy silent distance grew the Iceberg too.

IX.
Alien they seemed to be:
No mortal eye could see
The intimate welding of their later history,

X.
Or sign that they were bent
By paths coincident
On being anon twin halves of one august event,

XI.
Till the Spinner of the Years
Said "Now!" And each one hears,
And consummation comes, and jars two hemispheres.
                              —THOMAS HARDY (1840–1928)

Danny Deever

"What are the bugles blowin' for?" said Files-on-Parade.
"To turn you out, to turn you out," the Color Sergeant said.
"What makes you look so white, so white?" said Files-on-
    Parade.
"I'm dreadin' what I've got to watch," the Color Sergeant
    said.
  For they're hangin' Danny Deever, you can 'ear the dead
    march play,
  The regiment's in 'ollow square—they're hangin' him
    today;
  They've taken of his buttons off an' cut his stripes away,
  An' they're hangin' Danny Deever in the mornin'.

"What makes the rear-rank breathe so 'ard?" said Files-on-
    Parade.
"It's bitter cold, it's bitter cold," the Color Sergeant said.
"What makes that front-rank man fall down?" says Files-on-
    Parade.
"A touch o' sun, a touch o' sun," the Color Sergeant said.
  They are hangin' Danny Deever, they are marchin' of 'im
    round,
  They 'ave 'alted Danny Deever by 'is coffin on the ground:
  An' 'e'll swing in 'arf a minute for a sneakin', shootin'
    hound—

O they're hangin' Danny Deever in the mornin'!

" 'Is cot was right-'and cot to mine," said Files-on-Parade.
" 'E's sleepin' out an' far tonight," the Color Sergeant said.
"I've drunk 'is beer a score o' times,' said Files-on-Parade.
" 'E's drinkin' bitter beer alone," the Color Sergeant said.
They are hangin' Danny Deever, you must mark 'im to 'is
    place,
For 'e shot a comrade sleepin'—and you must look 'im in
    the face;
Nine 'undred of 'is county an' the regiment's disgrace,
While they're hangin' Danny Deever in the mornin'.

"What's that so black agin the sun?" said Files-on-Parade.
"It's Danny fightin' 'ard fur life," the Color Sergeant said.
"What's that that whimpers over'ead?" said Files-on-Parade.
"It's Danny's soul that's passin' now," the Color Sergeant
    said.
For they're done with Danny Deever, you can 'ear the
    quickstep play,
The regiment's in column, an' they're marchin' us away;
Ho! the young recruits are shakin', an' they'll want their
    beer today,
After hangin' Danny Deever in the mornin'.

—RUDYARD KIPLING (1865–1936)

Kubla Khan
Or, A Vision in a Dream

In Xanadu did Kubla Khan
A stately pleasure-dome decree:
Where Alph, the sacred river, ran
Through caverns measureless to man
        Down to a sunless sea.
So twice five miles of fertile ground
With walls and towers were girdled round:
And there were gardens bright with sinuous rills,
Where blossomed many an incense-bearing tree;
And here were forests ancient as the hills,
Enfolding sunny spots of greenery.

But oh! that deep romantic chasm which slanted
Down the green hill athwart a cedarn cover!

A savage place! as holy and enchanted
As e'er beneath a waning moon was haunted
By woman wailing for her demon-lover!
And from this chasm, with ceaseless turmoil seething,
As if this earth in fast thick pants were breathing,
A mighty fountain momently was forced;
Amid whose swift half-intermitted burst
Huge fragments vaulted like rebound hail,
Or chaffy grain beneath the thresher's flail:
And 'mid these dancing rocks at once and ever
It flung up momently the sacred river.
Five miles meandering with a mazy motion
Through wood and dale the sacred river ran,
Then reached the caverns measureless to man,
And sank in tumult to a lifeless ocean:
And 'mid this tumult Kubla heard from far
Ancestral voices prophesying war!

    The shadow of the dome of pleasure
    Floated midway on the waves;
    Where was heard the mingled measure
    From the fountain and the caves.
It was a miracle of rare device,
A sunny pleasure-dome with caves of ice!

    A damsel with a dulcimer
    In a vision once I saw:
    It was an Abyssinian maid,
    And on her dulcimer she played,
    Singing of Mount Abora.
    Could I revive within me
    Her symphony and song,
    To such a deep delight 'twould win me,
That with music loud and long,
I would build that dome in air,
That sunny dome! those caves of ice!
And all who heard should see them there,
And all should cry, Beware! Beware!
His flashing eyes, his floating hair!
Weave a circle round him thrice,
And close your eyes with holy dread,
For he on honey-dew hath fed,
And drunk the milk of Paradise.

—Samuel Taylor Coleridge (1772–1834)

The Ballad of the Harp-Weaver

"Son," said my mother,
    When I was knee-high,
"You've need of clothes to cover you,
    And not a rag have I.

"There's nothing in the house
    To make a boy breeches,
Nor shears to cut a cloth with
    Nor thread to take stitches.

"There's nothing in the house
    But a loaf-end of rye,
And a harp with a woman's head
    Nobody will buy."
    And she began to cry.

That was in the early fall.
    When came the late fall,
"Son," she said, "the sight of you
    Makes your mother's blood crawl,—

"Little skinny shoulder-blades
    Sticking through your clothes!
And where you'll get a jacket from
    God above knows!

"It's lucky for me, lad,
    Your daddy's in the ground,
And can't see the way I let
    His son go around!"
    And she made a queer sound.

That was in the late fall.
    When the winter came,
I'd not a pair of breeches
    Nor a shirt to my name.

I couldn't go to school,
    Or out of doors to play.
And all the other little boys
    Passed our way.

"Son," said my mother,
  "Come, climb into my lap,
And I'll chafe your little bones
  While you take a nap."

And, oh, but we were silly
  For half an hour or more,
Me with my long legs
  Dragging on the floor,

A-rock-rock-rocking
  To a mother-goose rhyme!
Oh, but we were happy
  For half an hour's time!

But there was I, a great boy,
  And what would folks say
To hear my mother singing me
  To sleep all day,
  In such a daft way?

Men say the winter
  Was bad that year;
Fuel was scarce,
  And food was dear.

A wind with a wolf's head
  Howled about our door,
And we burned up the chairs
  And sat upon the floor.

All that was left us
  Was a chair we couldn't break,
And the harp with a woman's head
  Nobody would take,
  For song or pity's sake.

The night before Christmas
  I cried with the cold,
I cried myself to sleep
  Like a two-year-old.

And in the deep night
   I felt my mother rise,
And stare down upon me
   With love in her eyes.

I saw my mother sitting
   On the one good chair,
A light falling on her
   From I couldn't tell where,

Looking nineteen,
   And not a day older,
And the harp with a woman's head
   Leaned against her shoulder.

Her thin fingers, moving
   In the thin, tall strings,
Were weav-weav-weaving
   Wonderful things.

Many bright threads,
   From where I couldn't see,
Were running through the harp-strings
   Rapidly,

And gold threads whistling
   Through my mother's hand.
I saw the web grow,
   And the pattern expand.

She wove a child's jacket,
   And when it was done
She laid it on the floor
   And wove another one.

She wove a red cloak
   So regal to see,
"She's made it for a king's son,"
   I said, "and not for me."
   But I knew it was for me.

She wove a pair of breeches
   Quicker than that!

She wove a pair of boots
   And a little cocked hat.

She wove a pair of mittens,
   She wove a little blouse,
She wove all night
   In the still, cold house.

She sang as she worked,
   And the harp-strings spoke;
Her voice never faltered,
   And the thread never broke.
   And when I awoke—

There sat my mother
   With the harp against her shoulder,
Looking nineteen
   And not a day older,

A smile about her lips,
   And a light about her head,
And her hands in the harp-strings
   Frozen dead.

And piled up beside her
   And toppling to the skies,
Were the clothes of a king's son,
   Just my size.
      —EDNA ST. VINCENT MILLAY (1892–1950)

Love

Cleopatra: *"If it be love indeed,
tell me how much."*
—WILLIAM SHAKESPEARE

The Passionate Shepherd to His Love

Come live with me, and be my love;
And we will all the pleasures prove
That hills and valleys, dales and fields,
Woods, or steepy mountain yields.

And we will sit upon the rocks,
Seeing the shepherds feed their flocks
By shallow rivers, to whose falls
Melodious birds sing madrigals.

And I will make thee beds of roses,
And a thousand fragrant posies;
A cap of flowers, and a kirtle
Embroidered all with leaves of myrtle;

A gown made of the finest wool
Which from our pretty lambs we pull;
Fair-lined slippers for the cold,
With buckles of the purest gold;

A belt of straw and ivy-buds,
With coral clasps and amber studs;
And if these pleasures may thee move,
Come live with me, and be my love.

The shepherd-swains shall dance and sing
For thy delight each May morning;
If these delights thy mind may move,
Then live with me, and be my love.

—CHRISTOPHER MARLOWE (1564–1593)

Love under the Republicans (Or Democrats)

Come live with me and be my love
And we will all the pleasures prove

madrigals, melodies; *kirtle*, skirt.

Of a marriage conducted with economy
In the Twentieth Century Anno Donomy.
We'll live in a dear little walk-up flat
With practically room to swing·a cat
And a potted cactus to give it hauteur
And a bathtub equipped with dark brown water.
We'll eat, without undue discouragement,
Foods low in cost but high in nouragement
And quaff with pleasure, while chatting wittily,
The peculiar wine of Little Italy.
We'll remind each other it's smart to be thrifty
And buy our clothes for something-fifty.
We'll bus for miles on holidays
For seats at depressing matinees,
And every Sunday we'll have a lark
And take a walk in Central Park.
And one of these days not too remote
You'll probably up and cut my throat.

—OGDEN NASH (b. 1902)

The Indian to His Love

The island dreams under the dawn
And great boughs drop tranquillity;
The peahens dance on a smooth lawn,
A parrot sways upon a tree,
Raging at his own image in the enamelled sea.

Here we will moor our lonely ship
And wander ever with woven hands,
Murmuring softly lip to lip,
Along the grass, along the sands,
Murmuring how far away are the unquiet lands:

How we alone of mortals are
Hid under quiet boughs apart,
While our love grows an Indian star,
A meteor of the burning heart,
One with the tide that gleams, the wings that gleam and dart,

The heavy boughs, the burnished dove
That moans and sighs a hundred days:

How when we die our shades will rove,
When eve has hushed the feathered ways,
With vapoury footsole by the water's drowsy blaze.

—WILLIAM BUTLER YEATS (1865–1939)

The Song of Solomon

The voice of my beloved! behold, he cometh leaping upon the mountains, skipping upon the hills.

My beloved is like a roe or a young hart: behold, he standeth behind our wall, he looketh forth at the windows, shewing himself through the lattice.

My beloved spake, and said unto me, Rise up, my love, my fair one, and come away.

For, lo, the winter is past, the rain is over *and* gone;

The flowers appear on the earth; the time of the singing *of birds* is come, and the voice of the turtle is heard in our land;

The fig tree putteth forth her green figs, and the vines *with* the tender grape give a *good* smell. Arise, my love, my fair one, and come away.

O my dove, *that art* in the clefts of the rock, in the secret *places* of the stairs, let me see thy countenance, let me hear thy voice; for sweet *is* thy voice, and thy countenance *is* comely.

Take us the foxes, the little foxes, that spoil the vines: for our vines *have* tender grapes.

My beloved *is* mine, and I *am* his: he feedeth among the lilies.

Until the day break, and the shadows flee away, turn, my beloved, and be thou like a roe or a young hart upon the mountains of the Bé-ther.

—THE SONG OF SOLOMON 2:8–17

Love's Philosophy

The fountains mingle with the river
And the rivers with the ocean;
The winds of heaven mix forever
With a sweet emotion;

Nothing in the world is single;
  All things by a law divine
In one another's being mingle—
  Why not I with thine?

See the mountains kiss high heaven,
  And the waves clasp one another;
No sister-flower would be forgiven
  If it disdain'd its brother:
And the sunlight clasps the earth,
  And the moonbeams kiss the sea—
What are all these kissings worth,
  If thou kiss not me?
—PERCY BYSSHE SHELLEY (1792–1822)

now air is air and thing is thing:no bliss

of heavenly earth beguiles our spirits,whose
miraculously disenchanted eyes

live the magnificent honesty of space.

Mountains are mountains now;skies now are skies—
and such a sharpening freedom lifts our blood
as if whole supreme this complete doubtless

universe we'd(and we alone had)made

—yes;or as if our souls,awakened from
summer's green trance,would not adventure soon
a deeper magic:that white sleep wherein
all human curiosity we'll spend
(gladly,as lovers must)immortal and

the courage to receive time's mightiest dream
—e. e. cummings (1894–1962)

"In a Drear-Nighted December"

In a drear-nighted December,
  Too happy, happy tree,
Thy branches ne'er remember
  Their green felicity:
The north cannot undo them
With a sleety whistle through them;
  Nor frozen thawings glue them
  From budding at the prime.

In a drear-nighted December,
  Too happy, happy brook,
  Thy bubblings ne'er remember
  Apollo's summer look;
But with a sweet forgetting,
They stay their crystal fretting,
Never, never petting
  About the frozen time.

Ah! would 'twere so with many
  A gentle girl and boy!
But were there ever any
  Writh'd not at passèd joy?
To know the change and feel it,
When there is none to heal it,
Nor numbèd sense to steel it—
  Was never said in rhyme.
                    —JOHN KEATS (1795–1821)

I Will Give My Love an Apple

I will give my love an apple without e'er a core;
I will give my love a dwelling without e'er a door;
I will give my love a palace wherein she may be,
And she may unlock it without e'er a key.

How can there be an apple without e'er a core?
How can there be a dwelling without e'er a door?
How can there be a palace wherein she may be,
That she may unlock it without e'er a key?

My head is an apple without e'er a core,
My mind is a dwelling without e'er a door,
My heart is the palace wherein she may be,
And she may unlock it without e'er a key.

I will give my love a cherry without e'er a stone,
I will give my love a chicken without e'er a bone,
I will give my love a ring, not a rent to be seen,
I will give my love a baby and no crying.

How can there be a cherry without e'er a stone?
How can there be a chicken without e'er a bone?
How can there be a ring, not a rent to be seen?
How can there be a baby and no crying?

When the cherry's in blossom it has no stone,
When the chicken's in the egg it has no bone,
When the ring's a-running, there's not a rent to be seen,
When the baby's a-getting, there's no crying.

—OLD BALLAD, AUTHOR UNKNOWN

Green Grow the Rushes, O

There's naught but care on every hand,
    In every hour that passes, O:
What signifies the life of man,
    And 'twere not for the lasses, O?

Refrain
    Green grow the rushes, O,
    Green grow the rushes, O,
    The sweetest hours that e'er are spent,
    Are spent among the lasses, O.

The worldly race may riches chase,
    And riches still may fly them, O;
And though at last they catch them fast,
    Their hearts may ne'er enjoy them, O.
Refrain

Give me a quiet hour at even,
    My arms about my dearie, O;
And worldly cares and worldly men,
    May all go topsyturvy, O.
Refrain

For you so prim you sneer at this,
    You're naught but senseless asses, O;
The wisest man the world e'er saw,
    He dearly loved the lasses, O.
Refrain

Old Nature swears the lovely dears
    Her noblest works she classes, O;
Her prentice hand she tried on man—
    And then she made the lasses, O.
Refrain

—ROBERT BURNS (1759–1796)

The Pity of Love

A pity beyond all telling
Is hid in the heart of love:
The folk who are buying and selling,
The clouds on their journey above,
The cold wet winds ever blowing,
And the shadowy hazel grove
Where mouse-grey waters are flowing,
Threaten the head that I love.

—WILLIAM BUTLER YEATS (1865–1939)

Shall I Compare Thee to a Summer's Day?

Shall I compare thee to a summer's day?
Thou are more lovely and more temperate.
Rough winds do shake the darling buds of May,
And summer's lease hath all too short a date.
Sometime too hot the eye of heaven shines,
And often is his gold complexion dimmed;
And every fair from fair sometimes declines,

By chance, or nature's changing course, untrimmed.
But thy eternal summer shall not fade
Nor lose possession of that fair thou ow'st,
Nor shall Death brag thou wand'rest in his shade
When in eternal lines to time thou grow'st.
  So long as men can breathe or eyes can see,
  So long lives this, and this gives life to thee.
           —WILLIAM SHAKESPEARE (1564–1616)

Let Me Not to the Marriage of True Minds

Let me not to the marriage of true minds
Admit impediments. Love is not love
Which alters when it alteration finds
Or bends with the remover to remove.
O, no! It is an ever-fixed mark
That looks on tempests and is never shaken;
It is the star to every wand'ring bark,
Whose worth's unknown, although his height be taken.
Love's not Time's fool, though rosy lips and cheeks
Within his bending sickle's compass come.
Love alters not with his brief hours and weeks,
But bears it out even to the edge of doom.
  If this be error and upon me proved,
  I never writ, nor no man ever loved.
           —WILLIAM SHAKESPEARE (1564–1616)

One Day I Wrote Her Name

One day I wrote her name upon the strand,
  but came the waves and washed it away:
  Again I wrote it with a second hand,
  but came the tide, and made my pains his prey.
Vain man, said she, that dost in vain assay
  a mortal thing so to immortalize,
  for I myself shall like to this decay,
  and eek my name be wipèd out likewise.
Not so, (quoth I) let baser things devise

bark, ship.

to die in dust, but you shall live by fame:
my verse your virtues rare shall eternize,
and in the heavens write your glorious name.
Where whenas death shall all the world subdue,
our love shall live, and later life renew.

—EDMUND SPENSER (1552?–1599)

Report of Health

I

I am alone tonight.
The wrong I have done you
sits like a sore beneath my thumb,
burns like a boil on my heart's left side.
I am unwell.

My viscera, long clenched in love of you,
have undergone a detested relaxation.

There is, within, a ghostly maze
of phantom tubes and nodules where
those citizens, our passions, flit; and here
like sunlight passing from a pattern of streets,
I feel your bright love leaving.

II

Another night. Today I am told,
dear friend, by another,
you seem happy and well.
Nothing could hurt me more.

How dare you be happy, you,
shaped so precisely for me,
my cup and my mirror—
how dare you disdain to betray,
by some disarray of your hair,
my being torn from you?

I would rather believe
that you knew your friend would come to me,
and so seemed well—
"not a hair out of place"—

like an actress blindly hurling a pose
into the fascinated darkness.

As for me, you are still the eyes of the air.
I travel from point to point in your presence.
Each unattended gesture hopes to catch your eye.

III

I may not write again. My voice
goes nowhere. Dear friend,
don't let me heal. Don't
worry, I am well.
I am happy
to dwell in a world whose Hell I will:

the doorway hints at your ghost
and a tiger pounces on my heart;
the lilac bush is a devil
inviting me into your hair.

—JOHN UPDIKE (b. 1932)

If Thou Must Love Me, Let It Be for Naught

If thou must love me, let it be for naught
Except for love's sake only. Do not say
"I love her for her smile—her look—her way
Of speaking gently—for a trick of thought
That falls in well with mine, and certes brought
A sense of pleasant ease on such a day"—
For these things in themselves, Belovèd, may
Be changed, or change for thee—and love, so wrought,
May be unwrought so. Neither love me for
Thine own dear pity's wiping my cheeks dry:
A creature might forget to weep, who bore
Thy comfort long, and lose thy love thereby!
But love me for love's sake, that evermore
Thou mayst love on, through love's eternity.

—ELIZABETH BARRETT BROWNING (1806–1861)

My Mistress' Eyes Are Nothing Like the Sun

My mistress' eyes are nothing like the sun;
Coral is far more red than her lips' red;
If snow be white, why then her breasts are dun;
If hairs be wires, black wires grow on her head.
I have seen roses damasked, red and white,
But no such roses see I in her cheeks;
And in some perfumes is there more delight
Than in the breath that from my mistress reeks.
I love to hear her speak, yet well I know
That music hath a far more pleasing sound.
I grant I never saw a goddess go:
My mistress, when she walks, treads on the ground.
   And yet, by Heaven, I think my love as rare
   As any she belied with false compare.
         —WILLIAM SHAKESPEARE (1564–1616)

Simplex Munditiis

Still to be neat, still to be drest,
As you were going to a feast;
Still to be powdered, still perfumed;
Lady, it is to be presumed,
Though art's hid causes are not found,
All is not sweet, all is not sound.

Give me a look, give me a face
That makes simplicity a grace;
Robes loosely flowing, hair as free.
Such sweet neglect more taketh me
Than all the adulteries of art;
They strike mine eyes, but not my heart.
         —BEN JONSON (1572–1637)

Delight in Disorder

A sweet disorder in the dress
Kindles in clothes a wantonness:
A lawn about the shoulders thrown
Into a fine distraction—
An erring lace, which here and there
Enthrals the crimson stomacher—
A cuff neglectful, and thereby
Ribands to flow confusedly—
A winning wave, deserving note,
In the tempestuous petticoat—
A careless shoe-string, in whose tie
I see a wild civility—
Do more bewitch me than when art
Is too precise in every part.

—ROBERT HERRICK (1591–1674)

No Loathesomenesse in Love

What I fancy, I approve,
No Dislike there is in love:
Be my Mistresse short or tall,
And distorted there-withall:
Be she likewise one of those,
That an *Acre* hath of Nose:
Be her forehead, and her eyes
Full of incongruities:
Be her cheeks so shallow too,
As to shew her *Tongue* wag through:
Be her lips ill hung, or set,
And her grinders black as jet;
Ha' she thinne haire, hath she none,
She's to be a *Paragon.*

—ROBERT HERRICK (1591–1674)

Cards and Kisses

Cupid and my Campaspe play'd
At cards for kisses—Cupid paid:

He stakes his quiver, bow, and arrows,
His mother's doves, and team of sparrows;
Loses them too; then down he throws
The coral of his lips, the rose
Growing on's cheek (but none knows how);
With these, the crystal of his brow,
And then the dimple of his chin:
All these did my Campaspe win.
At last he set her both his eyes—
She won, and Cupid blind did rise.
   O Love! has she done this for thee?
   What shall, alas! become of me?
                    —JOHN LYLY (1554?–1606)

The Constant Lover

Out upon it, I have loved
   Three whole days together!
And am like to love three more,
   If it prove fair weather.

Time shall moult away his wings,
   Ere he shall discover
In the whole wide world again
   Such a constant lover.

But the spite on't is, no praise
   Is due at all to me:
Love with me had made no stays,
   Had it any been but she.

Had it any been but she,
   And that very face,
There had been at least ere this
   A dozen dozen in her place.
                —SIR JOHN SUCKLING (1609–1642)

When I Was One-and-Twenty

When I was one-and-twenty
   I heard a wise man say,

"Give crowns and pounds and guineas
    But not your heart away;
Give pearls away and rubies
    But keep your fancy free."
But I was one-and-twenty,
    No use to talk to me.

When I was one-and-twenty
    I heard him say again,
"The heart out of the bosom
    Was never given in vain;
'Tis paid with sighs a plenty
    And sold for endless rue."
And I am two-and-twenty,
    And oh, 'tis true, 'tis true!
                    —A. E. HOUSMAN (1859–1936)

Song

Go, and catch a falling star,
    Get with child a mandrake root,
Tell me, where all past years are,
    Or who cleft the Devil's foot,
Teach me to hear mermaids singing,
    Or to keep off envy's stinging,
            And find
            What wind
Serves to advance an honest mind.

If thou beest borne to strange sights,
    Things invisible to see,
Ride ten thousand days and nights,
    Till age snow white hairs on thee,
Thou, when thou return'st, wilt tell me
All strange wonders that befell thee,
            And swear
            No where
Lives a woman true, and faire.

If thou findst one, let me know,
    Such a Pilgrimage were sweet;
Yet do not, I would not go,

Though at next door we might meet,
Though she were true, when you met her,
And last, till you write your letter,
    Yet she
    Will be
False, ere I come, to two, or three.
                        —JOHN DONNE (1573–1631)

Then and Now

Then

He loved her, and through many years,
Had paid his fair devoted court,
Until she wearied, and with sneers
Turned all his ardent love to sport.

That night within his chamber lone,
He long sat writing by his bed
A note in which his heart made moan
For love; the morning found him dead.

Now

Like him, a man of later day
Was jilted by the maid he sought,
And from his presence turned away,
Consumed by burning, bitter thought.

He sought his room to write—a curse
Like him before and die, I ween.
Ah no, he put his woes in verse,
And sold them to a magazine.
                        —PAUL LAURENCE DUNBAR (1872–1906)

The Indifferent

I can love both fair and brown;
Her whom abundance melts, and her whom want betrays;
Her who loves loneness best, and her who masks and plays;
Her whom the country formed, and whom the town;
Her who believes, and her who tries;
Her who still weeps with spongy eyes,
And her who is dry cork and never cries.

I can love her, and her, and you, and you;
I can love any, so she be not true.

Will no other vice content you?
Will it not serve your turn to do as did your mothers?
Or have you all old vices spent, and now would find out
    others?
Or doth a fear that men are true torment you?
O, we are not, be not you so;
Let me, and do you, twenty know.
Rob me, but bind me not, and let me go.
Must I, who came to travail thorough you,
Grow your fixed subject because you are true?

Venus heard me sigh this song,
And by love's sweetest part, variety, she swore,
She heard not this till now, and that it should be so no more.
She went, examined, and returned ere long,
And said, "Alas! some two or three
Poor heretics in love there be,
Which think to 'stablish dangerous constancy.
But I have told them, 'Since you will be true,
You shall be true to them who are false to you.' "

—JOHN DONNE (1573–1631)

Since There's No Help, Come Let Us Kiss and Part

Since there's no help, come let us kiss and part—
Nay, I have done, you get no more of me;
And I am glad, yea, glad with all my heart,
That thus so cleanly I myself can free.
Shake hands for ever, cancel all our vows,
And when we meet at any time again,
Be it not seen in either of our brows
That we one jot of former love retain.
Now at the last gasp of Love's latest breath,
When his pulse failing, Passion speechless lies,
When Faith is kneeling by his bed of death,
And Innocence is closing up his eyes,
    —Now if thou wouldst, when all have given him over,
    From death to life thou might'st him yet recover.

—MICHAEL DRAYTON (1563–1631)

Encouragement to a Lover

Why so pale and wan, fond lover?
    Prithee, why so pale?
Will, when looking well can't move her,
    Looking ill prevail?
    Prithee, why so pale?

Why so dull and mute, young sinner?
    Prithee, why so mute?
Will, when speaking well can't win her,
    Saying nothing do't?
    Prithee, why so mute?

Quit, quit, for shame! this will not move,
    This cannot take her;
If of herself she will not love,
    Nothing can make her:
    The Devil take her!
          —SIR JOHN SUCKLING (1609–1642)

The Cares o' Love

He
The cares o' Love are sweeter far
    Than onie other pleasure;
And if sae dear its sorrows are,
    Enjoyment, what a treasure!

She
I fear to try, I dare na try
    A passion sae ensnaring;
For light 's her heart and blithe 's her song
    That for nae man is caring.
          —ROBERT BURNS (1759–1796)

To the Virgins to Make Much of Time

Gather ye rosebuds while ye may,
  Old Time is still a-flying;
And this same flower that smiles to-day,
  To-morrow will be dying.

The glorious lamp of heaven, the sun,
  The higher he's a-getting,
The sooner will his race be run,
  And nearer he's to setting.

That age is best, which is the first,
  When youth and blood are warmer;
But being spent, the worse, and worst
  Times, still succeed the former.

Then be not coy, but use your time,
  And while ye may, go marry;
For, having lost but once your prime,
  You may forever tarry.
                        —ROBERT HERRICK (1591–1674)

To His Coy Mistress

Had we but world enough, and time,
This coyness, Lady, were no crime.
We would sit down and think which way
To walk and pass our long love's day.
Thou by the Indian Ganges' side
Shouldst rubies find; I by the tide
Of Humber would complain. I would
Love you ten years before the Flood,
And you should, if you please, refuse
Till the conversion of the Jews.
My vegetable love should grow
Vaster than empires, and more slow;
An hundred years should go to praise
Thine eyes and on thy forehead gaze;
Two hundred to adore each breast,

But thirty thousand to the rest;
An age at least to every part,
And the last age should show your heart.
For, Lady, you deserve this state,
Nor would I love at lower rate.

But at my back I always hear
Time's winged chariot hurrying near;
And yonder all before us lie
Deserts of vast eternity.
Thy beauty shall no more be found,
Nor, in thy marble vault, shall sound
My echoing song; then worms shall try
That long preserved virginity,
And your quaint honor turn to dust,
And into ashes all my lust:
The grave's a fine and private place,
But none, I think, do there embrace.

Now therefore, while the youthful hue
Sits on thy skin like morning dew,
And while thy willing soul transpires
At every pore with instant fires,
Now let us sport us while we may,
And now, like amorous birds of prey,
Rather at once our time devour
Than languish in his slow-chapped power.
Let us roll all our strength and all
Our sweetness up into one ball,
And tear our pleasures with rough strife
Thorough the iron gates of life:
Thus, though we cannot make our sun
Stand still, yet we will make him run.

—Andrew Marvell (1621–1678)

Engaged

Stretched out on the grass
a boy and a girl.
Sucking their oranges, giving their kisses
like waves exchanging foam.

Stretched out on the beach
a boy and a girl.

Sucking their limes, giving their kisses,
like clouds exchanging foam.

Stretched out underground
a boy and a girl.
Saying nothing, never kissing,
giving silence for silence.

—OCTAVIO PAZ (b. 1914)
TRANSLATED BY MURIEL RUKEYSER (b. 1913)

Mercury's Song to Phaedra

Fair *Iris* I love, and hourly I die,
But not for a Lip, nor a languishing Eye:
She's fickle and false, and there we agree;
For I am as false, and as fickle as she:
We neither believe what either can say;
And, neither believing, we neither betray.

'Tis civil to swear, and say things of course;
We mean not the taking for better for worse.
When present, we love; when absent, agree:
I think not of *Iris*, nor *Iris* of me:
The Legend of Love no Couple can find
So easie to part, or so equally join'd.

—JOHN DRYDEN (1631–1700)

This Is Just to Say

I have eaten
the plums
that were in
the icebox

and which
you were probably
saving
for breakfast

Forgive me
they were delicious
so sweet
and so cold.
—WILLIAM CARLOS WILLIAMS (1883–1963)

A Young Wife

The pain of loving you
Is almost more than I can bear.

I walk in fear of you.
The darkness starts up where
You stand, and the night comes through
Your eyes when you look at me.

Ah, never before did I see
The shadows that live in the sun!

Now every tall glad tree
Turns round its back to the sun
And looks down on the ground, to see
The shadow it used to shun.

At the foot of each glowing thing
A night lies looking up.

Oh, and I want to sing
And dance, but I can't lift up
My eyes from the shadows: dark
They lie split round the cup.

What is it?—Hark
The faint fine seethe in the air!

Like the seething sound in a shell!
It is death still seething where
The wild-flower shakes its bell
And the skylark twinkles blue—

The pain of loving you
Is almost more than I can bear.
                    —D. H. LAWRENCE (1885–1930)

Sonnet from Modern Love

By this he knew she wept with waking eyes:
That, at his hand's light quiver by her head,
The strange low sobs that shook their common bed,
Were called into her with a sharp surprise,
And strangled mute, like little gaping snakes,
Dreadfully venomous to him. She lay
Stone-still, and the long darkness flowed away
With muffled pulses. Then, as midnight makes
Her giant heart of Memory and Tears
Drink the pale drug of silence, and so beat
Sleep's heavy measure, they from head to feet
Were moveless, looking through their dead black years
By vain regret scrawled over the blank wall.
Like sculptured effigies they might be seen
Upon their marriage tomb, the sword between,
Each wishing for the sword that severs all.

—GEORGE MEREDITH (1828–1909)

If There Be Sorrow

If there be sorrow
let it be
for things undone . . .
undreamed
   unrealized
      unattained
to these add one:
Love withheld . . .
. . . restrained

—MARI EVANS

When We Two Parted

When we two parted
   In silence and tears,
Half broken-hearted

To sever for years,
    Pale grew thy cheek and cold,
        Colder thy kiss;
    Truly that hour foretold
        Sorrow to this.

The dew of the morning
    Sunk chill on my brow—
It felt like the warning
    Of what I feel now.
Thy vows are all broken,
    And light is thy fame:
I hear thy name spoken,
    And share in its shame.

They name thee before me,
    A knell to mine ear;
A shudder comes o'er me—
    Why wert thou so dear?
They know not I knew thee,
    Who knew thee too well:
Long, long shall I rue thee,
    Too deeply to tell.

In secret we met—
    In silence I grieve,
That thy heart could forget,
    Thy spirit deceive.
If I should meet thee
    After long years,
How should I greet thee?
    With silence and tears.

—George Gordon Byron, Lord Byron (1788–1824)

A Poison Tree

I was angry with my friend:
I told my wrath, my wrath did end.
I was angry with my foe:
I told it not, my wrath did grow.

And I water'd it in fears,
Night & morning with my tears;
And I sunned it with smiles,
And with soft deceitful wiles.

And it grew both day and night,
Till it bore an apple bright;
And my foe beheld it shine,
And he knew that it was mine,

And into my garden stole
When the night had veil'd the pole:
In the morning glad I see
My foe outstretch'd beneath the tree.
            —WILLIAM BLAKE (1757–1827)

Two Friends

I have something to tell you.
I'm listening.
I'm dying.
I'm sorry to hear.
I'm growing old.
It's terrible.
It is; I thought you should know.
Of course and I'm sorry. Keep in touch.
I will and you too.
And let know what's new.
Certainly, though it can't be much.
And stay well.
And you too.
And go slow.
And you too.
            —DAVID IGNATOW (b. 1914)

Generation

"It's all that the young can do for the old, to shock them and keep them up to date."
—George Bernard Shaw

The Lost Children

Two little girls, one fair, one dark,
One alive, one dead, are running hand in hand
Through a sunny house. The two are dressed
In red and white gingham, with puffed sleeves and sashes.
They run away from me . . . But I am happy;
When I wake I feel no sadness, only delight.
I've seen them again, and I am comforted
That, somewhere, they still are.

It is strange
To carry inside you someone else's body;
To know it before it's born;
To see at last that it's a boy or girl, and perfect;
To bathe it and dress it; to watch it
Nurse at your breast, till you almost know it
Better than you know yourself—better than it knows itself.
You own it as you made it.
You are the authority upon it.

But as the child learns
To take care of herself, you know her less.
Her accidents, adventures are her own,
You lose track of them. Still, you know more
About her than anyone *except* her.

Little by little the child in her dies.
You say, "I have lost a child, but gained a friend."
You feel yourself gradually discarded.
She argues with you or ignores you
Or is kind to you. She who begged to follow you
Anywhere, just so long as it was you,
Finds follow the leader no more fun.
She makes few demands; you are grateful for the few.

The young person who writes once a week
Is the authority upon herself.
She sits in my living room and shows her husband
My albums of her as a child. He enjoys them
And makes fun of them. I look too

And I realize the girl in the matching blue
Mother-and-daughter dress, the fair one carrying
The tin lunch box with the half-pint thermos bottle
Or training her pet duck to go down the slide
Is lost just as the dark one, who is dead, is lost.
But the world in which the two wear their flared coats
And the hats that match, exists so uncannily
That, after I've seen its pictures for an hour,
I believe in it: the bandage coming loose
One has in the picture of the other's birthday,
The castles they are building, at the beach for asthma.
I look at them and all the old sure knowledge
Floods over me, when I put the album down
I keep saying inside: "I *did* know those children.
I braided those braids. I was driving the car
The day that she stepped in the can of grease
We were taking to the butcher for our ration points.
I *know* those children. I know all about them.
Where are they?"

I stare at her and try to see some sign
Of the child she was. I can't believe there isn't any.
I tell her foolishly, pointing at the picture,
That I keep wondering where she is.
She tells me, "Here I am."

                  Yes, and the other
Isn't dead, but has everlasting life . . .

The girl from next door, the borrowed child,
Said to me the other day, "You like children so much,
Don't you want to have some of your own?"
I couldn't believe that she could say it.
I thought: "Surely you can look at me and see them."

When I see them in my dreams I feel such joy.
If I could dream of them every night!

When I think of my dream of the little girls
It's as if we were playing hide-and-seek.
The dark one
Looks at me longingly, and disappears;
The fair one stays in sight, just out of reach
No matter where I reach. I am tired
As a mother who's played all day, some rainy day.

I don't want to play it any more, I don't want to,
But the child keeps on playing, so I play.
                    —RANDALL JARRELL (1914–1965)

On My First Son

Farewell, thou child of my right hand, and joy;
    My sin was too much hope of thee, loved boy.
Seven years thou wert lent to me, and I thee pay,
    Exacted by thy fate, on the just day.
Oh, could I lose all father now! For why
    Will man lament the state he should envy?
To have so soon 'scaped world's and flesh's rage,
    And if no other misery, yet age!
Rest in soft peace, and asked, say, Here doth lie
    Ben Jonson his best piece of poetry.
For whose sake henceforth all his vows be such,
    As what he loves may never like too much.
                    —BEN JONSON (1572–1637)

The Goodnight

He stood still by her bed
Watching his daughter breathe,
The dark and silver head,
The fingers curled beneath,
And thought: Though she may have
Intelligence and charm
And luck, they will not save
Her life from every harm.

The lives of children are
Dangerous to their parents
With fire, water, air,
And other accidents;
And some, for a child's sake,
Anticipating doom,
Empty the world to make
The world safe as a room.

Who could endure the pain
That was Laocoön's?
Twisting, he saw again
In the same coil his sons.
Plumed in his father's skill,
Young Icarus flew higher
Toward the sun, until
He fell in rings of fire.

A man who cannot stand
Children's perilous play,
With lifted voice and hand
Drives the children away.
Out of sight, out of reach,
The tumbling children pass;
He sits on an empty beach,
Holding an empty glass.

Who said that tenderness
Will turn the heart to stone?
May I endure her weakness
As I endure my own.
Better to say goodnight
To breathing flesh and blood
Each night as though the night
Were always only good.

—LOUIS SIMPSON (b. 1923)

My Papa's Waltz

The whiskey on your breath
Could make a small boy dizzy;
But I hung on like death:
Such waltzing was not easy.

We romped until the pans
Slid from the kitchen shelf;
My mother's countenance
Could not unfrown itself.

The hand that held my wrist
Was battered on one knuckle;

At every step you missed
My right ear scraped a buckle.

You beat time on my head
With a palm caked hard by dirt,
Then waltzed me off to bed
Still clinging to your shirt.
—THEODORE ROETHKE (1908–1963)

Europe and America

My father brought the emigrant bundle
of desperation and worn threads,
that in anxiety as he stumbles
tumble out distractedly;
while I am bedded upon soft green money
that grows like grass. Thus,
between my father who lives on a bed of anguish
for his daily bread, and I who tear money
at leisure by the roots,
where I lie in sun or shade,
a vast continent of breezes, storms to him,
shadows, darkness to him, small lakes,
difficult channels to him, and hills,
mountains to him, lie between us.

My father comes of a hell
where bread and man have been kneaded
and baked together. You have heard the scream
as the knife fell; while I have slept
as guns pounded on the shore.
—DAVID IGNATOW (b. 1914)

Laid in My Quiet Bed

Laid in my quiet bed, in study as I were,
I saw within my troubled head a heap of thoughts appear;
And every thought did shew so lively in mine eyes,
That now I sighed, and then I smiled, as cause of thought
    did rise.

I saw the little boy in thought how oft that he
Did wish of God, to scape the rod, a tall young man to be.
The young man eke that feels his bones with pains opprest,
How he would be a rich old man, to live and lie at rest.
The rich old man that sees his end draw on so sore,
How he would be a boy again, to live so much the more.
Whereat full oft I smiled, to see how all these three,
From boy to man, from man to boy, would chop and change
    degree . . .
        —HENRY HOWARD, EARL OF SURREY (1517?–1547)

Home after Three Months Away

Gone now the baby's nurse,
a lioness who ruled the roost
and made the Mother cry.
She used to tie
gobbets of porkrind in bowknots of gauze—
three months they hung like soggy toast
on our eight foot magnolia tree,
and helped the English sparrows
weather a Boston winter.
Three months, three months!
Is Richard now himself again?
Dimpled with exaltation,
my daughter holds her levee in the tub.
Our noses rub,
each of us pats a stringy lock of hair—
they tell me nothing's gone.
Though I am forty-one,
not forty now, the time I put away
was child's-play. After thirteen weeks
my child still dabs her cheeks
to start me shaving. When
we dress her in sky-blue corduroy,
she changes to a boy,
and floats my shaving brush
and washcloth in the flush . . .
Dearest, I cannot loiter here
in lather like a polar bear.
Recuperating, I neither spin nor toil.

Three stories down below,
a choreman tends our coffin's length of soil,
and seven horizontal tulips blow.
Just twelve months ago,
these flowers were pedigreed
imported Dutchmen; now no one need
distinguish them from weed.
Bushed by the late spring snow,
they cannot meet
another year's snowballing enervation.

I keep no rank nor station.
Cured, I am frizzled, stale and small.
—ROBERT LOWELL (b. 1917)

Why Did the Children Put Beans in Their Ears?

"Why did the children
  put beans in their ears
  when the one thing we told the children
  they must not do
  was put beans in their ears?

"Why did the children
  pour molasses on the cat
  when the one thing we told the children
  they must not do
  was pour molasses on the cat?"
—CARL SANDBURG (1878–1967)

Nikki-Roasa

childhood rememberances are always a drag
if you're Black
you always remember things like living in Woodlawn
with no inside toilet
and if you become famous or something
they never talk about how happy you were to have your
    mother
all to yourself and

how good the water felt when you got your bath from one
    of those
big tubs that folk in chicago barbecue in
and somehow when you talk about home
it never gets across how much you
understood their feelings
as the whole family attended meetings about Hollydale
and even though you remember
your biographers never understand
your father's pain as he sells his stock
and another dream goes
and though you're poor it isn't poverty that
concerns you
and though they fought a lot
it isn't your father's drinking that makes any difference
but only that everybody is together and you
and your sister have happy birthdays and very good christ-
masses and I really hope no white person ever has cause to
write about me because they never understand Black love
is Black wealth and they'll probably talk about my hard
childhood and never understand that all the while I was
quite happy

                      —NIKKI GIOVANNI (b. 1943)

Rough

My parents kept me from children who were rough
Who threw words like stones and who wore torn clothes.
Their thighs showed through rags. They ran in the street
And climbed cliffs and stripped by the country streams.

I feared more than tigers their muscles like iron
Their jerking hands and their knees tight on my arms.
I feared the salt coarse pointing of those boys
Who copied my lisp behind me on the road.

They were lithe, they sprang out behind hedges
Like dogs to bark at my world. They threw mud
While I looked the other way, pretending to smile.
I longed to forgive them, but they never smiled.

                      —STEPHEN SPENDER (b. 1909)

The Leaden-Eyed

Let not young souls be smothered out before
They do quaint deeds and fully flaunt their pride.
It is the world's one crime its babes grow dull,
Its poor are oxlike, limp, and leaden-eyed.
Not that they starve, but starve so dreamlessly,
Not that they sow, but that they seldom reap,
Not that they serve, but have no gods to serve;
Not that they die, but that they die like sheep.
                    —VACHEL LINDSAY (1879–1931)

How Soon Hath Time the Subtle Thief of Youth

How soon hath time the subtle thief of youth,
Stol'n on his wing my three-and-twentieth year!
My hasting days fly on with full career,
But my late spring no bud or blossom show'th.
Perhaps my semblance might deceive the truth
That I to manhood am arrived so near;
And inward ripeness doth much less appear,
That some more timely-happy spirits indu'th.
Yet be it less or more, or soon or slow,
It shall be still in strictest measure ev'n
To that same lot, however mean or high,
Toward which Time leads me, and the will of Heav'n;
All is, if I have grace to use it so,
As ever in my great task-master's eye.
                    —JOHN MILTON (1608–1674)

That Time of Year Thou Mayst in Me Behold

That time of year thou mayst in me behold
When yellow leaves, or none, or few, do hang
Upon those boughs which shake against the cold,
Bare ruined choirs, where late the sweet birds sang.
In me thou see'st the twilight of such day
As after sunset fadeth in the west,

Which by and by black night doth take away,
Death's second self, that seals up all in rest.
In me thou see'st the glowing of such fire
That on the ashes of his youth doth lie,
As the death-bed whereon it must expire,
Consumed with that which it was nourished by.
   This thou perceivest, which makes thy love more strong,
    To love that well which thou must leave ere long.
           —WILLIAM SHAKESPEARE (1564–1616)

Do Not Go Gentle into That Good Night

Do not go gentle into that good night,
Old age should burn and rave at close of day;
Rage, rage against the dying of the light.

Though wise men at their end know dark is right,
Because their words had forked no lightning they
Do not go gentle into that good night.

Good men, the last wave by, crying how bright
Their frail deeds might have danced in a green bay,
Rage, rage against the dying of the light.

Wild men who caught and sang the sun in flight,
And learn, too late, they grieved it on its way,
Do not go gentle into that good night.

Grave men, near death, who see with blinding sight
Blind eyes could blaze like meteors and be gay,
Rage, rage against the dying of the light.

And you, my father, there on the sad height,
Curse, bless, me now with your fierce tears, I pray.
Do not go gentle into that good night.
Rage, rage against the dying of the light.
           —DYLAN THOMAS (1914–1953)

for prodigal read generous

for prodigal read generous
—for youth read age—
read for sheer wonder mere surprise
(then turn the page)

contentment read for ecstasy
—for poem prose—
caution for curiosity
(and close your eyes)
—e. e. cummings (1894–1962)

Rabbi Ben Ezra

I

Grow old along with me!
The best is yet to be,
The last of life, for which the first was made:
Our times are in His hand
Who saith "A whole I planned,
"Youth shows but half; trust God: see all nor be afraid!"

II

Not that, amassing flowers,
Youth sighed "Which rose make ours,
"Which lily leave and then as best recall?"
Not that, admiring stars,
It yearned "Nor Jove, nor Mars;
"Mine be some figured flame which blends, transcends them
      all!"

III

Not for such hopes and fears
Annulling youth's brief years,
Do I remonstrate: folly wide the mark!
Rather I prize the doubt
Low kinds exist without,
Finished and finite clods, untroubled by a spark.

IV

Poor vaunt of life indeed,
Were man but formed to feed
On joy, to solely seek and find and feast:
Such feasting ended, then
As sure an end to men;
Irks care the crop-full bird? Frets doubt the maw-crammed
beast?

V

Rejoice we are allied
To That which doth provide
And not partake, effect and not receive!
A spark disturbs our clod;
Nearer we hold of God
Who gives, than of His tribes that take, I must believe.

VI

Then, welcome each rebuff
That turns earth's smoothness rough,
Each sting that bids nor sit nor stand but go!
Be our joys three-parts pain!
Strive, and hold cheap the strain;
Learn, nor account the pang; dare, never grudge the throe!

VII

For thence,—a paradox
Which comforts while it mocks,—
Shall life succeed in that it seems to fail:
What I aspired to be,
And was not, comforts me:
A brute I might have been, but would not sink i' the scale.

VIII

What is he but a brute
Whose flesh has soul to suit,
Whose spirit works lest arms and legs want play?
To man, propose this test—
Thy body at its best,
How far can that project thy soul on its lone way?

IX

Yet gifts should prove their use:
I own the Past profuse

Of power each side, perfection every turn:
    Eyes, ears took in their dole,
    Brain treasured up the whole;
Should not the heart beat once "How good to live and learn?"

X

    Not once beat "Praise be Thine!
    "I see the whole design,
"I, who saw power, see now love perfect too:
    "Perfect I call Thy plan:
    "Thanks that I was a man!
"Maker, remake, complete,—I trust what Thou shalt do!"

XI

    For pleasant is this flesh;
    Our soul, in its rose-mesh
Pulled ever to the earth, still yearns for rest;
    Would we some prize might hold
    To match those manifold
Possessions of the brute,—gain most, as we did best!

XII

    Let us not always say
    "Spite of this flesh to-day
"I strove, made head, gained ground upon the whole!"
    As the bird wings and sings,
    Let us cry "All good things
"Are ours, nor soul helps flesh more, now, than flesh helps
        soul!"

XIII

    Therefore I summon age
    To grant youth's heritage,
Life's struggle having so far reached its term:
    Thence shall I pass, approved
    A man, for aye removed
From the developed brute; a god though in the germ.

XIV

    And I shall thereupon
    Take rest, ere I be gone
Once more on my adventure brave and new:
    Fearless and unperplexed,

When I wage battle next,
What weapons to select, what armour to indue.

XV

Youth ended, I shall try
My gain or loss thereby;
Leave the fire ashes, what survives is gold:
And I shall weigh the same,
Give life its praise or blame:
Young, all lay in dispute; I shall know, being old.

XVI

For note, when evening shuts,
A certain moment cuts
The deed off, calls the glory from the grey:
A whisper from the west
Shoots—"Add this to the rest,
"Take it and try its worth: here dies another day."

XVII

So, still within this life,
Though lifted o'er its strife,
Let me discern, compare, pronounce at last,
"This rage was right i' the main,
"That acquiescence vain:
"The Future I may face now I have proved the Past."

XVIII

For more is not reserved
To man, with soul just nerved
To act to-morrow what he learns to-day:
Here, work enough to watch
The Master work, and catch
Hints of the proper craft, tricks of the tool's true play.

XIX

As it was better, youth
Should strive, through acts uncouth,
Toward making, than repose on aught found made:
So, better, age, exempt
From strife, should know, than tempt
Further. Thou waitedest age: wait death nor be afraid!

XX

Enough now, if the Right
And Good and Infinite
Be named here, as thou callest thy hand thine own,
With knowledge absolute,
Subject to no dispute
From fools that crowded youth, nor let thee feel alone.

XXI

Be there, for once and all,
Severed great minds from small,
Announced to each his station in the Past!
Was I, the world arraigned,
Were they, my soul disdained,
Right? Let age speak the truth and give us peace at last!

XXII

Now, who shall arbitrate?
Ten men love what I hate,
Shun what I follow, slight what I receive;
Ten, who in ears and eyes
Match me: we all surmise,
They this thing, and I that: whom shall my soul believe?

XXIII

Not on the vulgar mass
Called "work," must sentence pass,
Things done, that took the eye and had the price;
O'er which, from level stand,
The low world laid its hand,
Found straightway to its mind, could value in a trice:

XXIV

But all, the world's coarse thumb
And finger failed to plumb,
So passed in making up the main account;
All instincts immature,
All purposes unsure,
That weighed not as his work, yet swelled the man's amount:

XXV

Thoughts hardly to be packed
Into a narrow act,

Fancies that broke through language and escaped;
  All I could never be,
  All, men ignored in me,
This, I was worth to God, whose wheel the pitcher shaped.

XXVI

  Ay, note that Potter's wheel,
  That metaphor! and feel
Why time spins fast, why passive lies our clay,—
  Thou, to whom fools propound,
  When the wine makes its round,
"Since life fleets, all is change; the Past gone, seize to-day!"

XXVII

  Fool! All that is, at all,
  Lasts ever, past recall;
Earth changes, but thy soul and God stand sure:
  What entered into thee,
  That was, is, and shall be:
Time's wheel runs back or stops: Potter and clay endure.

XXVIII

  He fixed thee mid this dance
  Of plastic circumstance,
This Present, thou, forsooth, wouldst fain arrest:
  Machinery just meant
  To give thy soul its bent,
Try thee and turn thee forth, sufficiently impressed.

XXIX

  What though the earlier grooves
  Which ran the laughing loves
Around thy base, no longer pause and press?
  What though, about thy rim,
  Skull-things in order grim
Grow out, in graver mood, obey the sterner stress?

XXX

  Look not thou down but up!
  To uses of a cup,
The festal board, lamp's flash and trumpet's peal,
  The new wine's foaming flow,
  The Master's lips a-glow!

Thou, heaven's consummate cup, what need'st thou with
      earth's wheel?

XXXI

    But I need, now as then,
    Thee, God, who mouldest men;
And since, not even while the whirl was worst,
    Did I,—to the wheel of life
    With shapes and colours rife,
Bound dizzily,—mistake my end, to slake Thy thirst:

XXXII

    So, take and use Thy work:
    Amend what flaws may lurk,
What strain o' the stuff, what warpings past the aim!
    My times be in Thy hand!
    Perfect the cup as planned!
Let age approve of youth, and death complete the same!
        —ROBERT BROWNING (1812–1889)

The Slow Starter

    A watched clock never moves, they said:
    Leave it alone and you'll grow up.
    Nor will the sulking holiday train
    Start sooner if you stamp your feet.
        He left the clock to go its way;
        The whistle blew, the train went gay.

    Do not press me so, she said;
    Leave me alone and I will write
    But not just yet, I am sure you know
    The problem. Do not count the days.
        He left the calendar alone;
        The postman knocked, no letter came.

    O never force the pace, they said;
    Leave it alone, you have lots of time,
    Your kind of work is none the worse
    For slow maturing. Do not rush.
        He took their tip, he took his time,
        And found his time and talent gone.
    Oh you have had your chance, It said;

Left it alone and it was one.
Who said a watched clock never moves?
Look at it now. Your chance was I.
He turned and saw the accusing clock
Race like a torrent round a rock.

—LOUIS MacNEICE (1907–1963)

Humor

"Though it was really one laugh with a tear in the middle, I counted it as two."
—JAMES M. BARRIE

The Mad Gardener's Song

He thought he saw an Elephant,
    That practiced on a fife:
He looked again, and found it was
    A letter from his wife.
"At length I realize," he said,
    "The bitterness of Life!"

He thought he saw a Buffalo
    Upon the chimney-piece:
He looked again, and found it was
    His Sister's Husband's Niece.
"Unless you leave this house," he said,
    "I'll send for the Police!"

He thought he saw a Rattlesnake
    That questioned him in Greek:
He looked again, and found it was
    The Middle of Next Week.
"The one thing I regret," he said,
    "Is that it cannot speak!"

He thought he saw a Banker's Clerk
    Descending from the bus:
He looked again, and found it was
    A Hippopotamus.
"If this should stay to dine," he said,
    "There won't be much for us!"

He thought he saw a Kangaroo
    That worked a coffee-mill:
He looked again, and found it was
    A Vegetable-Pill.
"Were I to swallow this," he said,
    "I should be very ill!"

He thought he saw a Coach-and-Four
    That stood beside his bed:
He looked again, and found it was
    A Bear without a Head.

"Poor thing," he said, "poor silly thing!
  It's waiting to be fed!"

He thought he saw an Albatross
    That fluttered round the lamp:
He looked again, and found it was
    A Penny-Postage-Stamp.
"You'd best be getting home," he said,
    "The nights are very damp!"

He thought he saw a Garden-Door
    That opened with a key:
He looked again, and found it was
    A Double Rule of Three:
"And all its mystery," he said,
    "Is clear as day to me!"

He thought he saw an Argument
    That proved he was the Pope:
He looked again, and found it was
    A Bar of Mottled Soap.
"A fact so dread," he faintly said,
    "Extinguishes all hope!"

—LEWIS CARROLL (1832–1898)

The Sycophantic Fox and the Gullible Raven

A raven sat upon a tree,
    And not a word he spoke, for
His beak contained a piece of Brie,
    Or, maybe, it was Roquefort.
        We'll make it any kind you please—
        At all events it was a cheese.

Beneath the tree's umbrageous limb
    A hungry fox sat smiling;
He saw the raven watching him,
    And spoke in words beguiling:
        "J'admire," said he, "ton beau plumage,"
        (The which was simply persiflage.)

Two things there are, no doubt you know,
    To which a fox is used:
A rooster that is bound to crow,
      A crow that's bound to roost:
        And whichsoever he espies
        He tells the most unblushing lies.

"Sweet fowl," he said, "I understand
    You're more than merely natty,
I hear you sing to beat the band
      And Adelina Patti.
        Pray render with your liquid tongue
        A bit from *Gotterdammerung*."

This subtle speech was aimed to please
    The crow, and it succeeded;
He thought no bird in all the trees
      Could sing as well as he did.
        In flattery completely doused,
        He gave the "Jewel Song" from *Faust*.

But gravitation's law, of course,
    As Isaac Newton showed it,
Exerted on the cheese its force,
      And elsewhere soon bestowed it.
        In fact, there is no need to tell
        What happened when to earth it fell.

I blush to add that when the bird
    Took in the situation
He said one brief, emphatic word,
      Unfit for publication.
        The fox was greatly startled, but
        He only sighed and answered "Tut."

The Moral is: A fox is bound
    To be a shameless sinner.
And also: when the cheese comes round
      You know it's after dinner.
        But (what is only known to few)
        The fox is after dinner, too.
           —GUY WETMORE CARRYL (1873–1904)

Nightmare

When you're lying awake with a dismal headache, and repose
    is taboo'd by anxiety,
I conceive you may use any language you choose to indulge
    in, without impropriety;
For your brain is on fire—the bedclothes conspire of usual
    slumber to plunder you:
First your counterpane goes, and uncovers your toes, and
    your sheet slips demurely from under you;
Then the blanketing tickles—you feel like mixed pickles—so
    terribly sharp is the pricking,
And you're hot, and you're cross, and you tumble and toss
    till there's nothing 'twixt you and the ticking.
Then the bedclothes all creep to the ground in a heap, and
    you pick 'em all up in a tangle;
Next your pillow resigns and politely declines to remain at its
    usual angle!
Well, you get some repose in the form of a doze, with hot
    eyeballs and head ever aching,
But your slumbering teems with such horrible dreams that
    you'd very much better be waking;
For you dream you are crossing the Channel, and tossing
    about in a steamer from Harwich—
Which is something between a large bathing machine and a
    very small second-class carriage—
And you're giving a treat (penny ice and cold meat) to a
    party of friends and relations—
They're a ravenous horde—and they all came on board at
    Sloane Square and South Kensington Stations.
And bound on that journey you find your attorney (who
    started that morning from Devon);
He's a bit undersized, and you don't feel surprised when he
    tells you he's only eleven.
Well, you're driving like mad with this singular lad (by-the-
    bye the ship's now a four-wheeler),
And you're playing round games, and he calls you bad names
    when you tell him that 'ties pay the dealer';
But this you can't stand, so you throw up your hand, and you
    find you're as cold as an icicle,
In your shirt and your socks (the black silk with gold clocks),
    crossing Salisbury Plain on a bicycle:

And he and the crew are on bicycles too—which they've
    somehow or other invested in—
And he's telling the tars, all the particu*lars* of a company
    he's interested in—
It's a scheme of devices, to get at low prices, all goods from
    cough mixtures to cables
(Which tickled the sailors) by treating retailers, as though
    they were all vege*tables*—
You get a good spadesman to plant a small tradesman, (first
    take off his boots with a boot-tree),
And his legs will take root, and his fingers will shoot, and
    they'll blossom and bud like a fruit-tree—
From the greengrocer tree you gets grapes and green pea,
    cauliflower, pineapple, and cranberries,
While the pastrycook plant, cherry brandy will grant, apple
    puffs, and three-corners, and banberries—
The shares are a penny, and ever so many are taken by
    Rothschild and Baring,
And just as a few are allotted to you, you awake with a
    shudder despairing—
You're a regular wreck, with a crick in your neck, and no
    wonder you snore, for your head's on the floor, and
    you've needles and pins from your soles to your shins,
    and your flesh is a-creep for your left leg's asleep, and
    you've cramp in your toes, and a fly on your nose, and
    some fluff in your lung, and a feverish tongue, and a
    thirst that's intense, and a general sense that you haven't
    been sleeping in clover;
But the darkness has passed, and it's daylight at last, and the
    night has been long—ditto ditto my song—and thank
    goodness they're both of them over!

—W. S. GILBERT (1836–1911)

To an Artist

Dear ———, I 'll gie ye some advice,
    You 'll tak it no uncivil:
You shouldna paint at angels, man,
    But try and paint the Devil.

To paint an angel's kittle wark,
    Wi' Nick there 's little danger:

You 'll easy draw a lang-kent face,
But no sae weel a stranger.
—ROBERT BURNS (1759–1796)

Evidence Read at the Trial of the Knave of Hearts

They told me you had been to her,
And mentioned me to him:
She gave me a good character,
But said I could not swim.

He sent them word I had not gone,
(We know it to be true):
If she should push the matter on,
What would become of you?

I gave her one, they gave him two,
You gave us three or more;
They all returned from him to you,
Though they were mine before.

If I or she should chance to be
Involved in this affair,
He trusts to you to set them free,
Exactly as we were.

My notion was that you had been
(Before she had this fit)
An obstacle that came between
Him, and ourselves, and it.

Don't let him know she liked them best,
For this must ever be
A secret kept from all the rest,
Between yourself and me.
—LEWIS CARROLL (1832–1898)

lang-kent, well-known.

Death at Suppertime

Between the dark and the daylight,
  When the night is beginning to lower,
Comes a pause in the day's occupation,
  That is known as the Children's Hour.

That endeth the skipping and skating,
  The giggles, the tantrums, and tears,
When, the innocent voices abating,
  Alert grow the innocent ears.

The little boys leap from the stairways,
  Girls lay down their dolls on the dot,
For promptly at five o'er the airways
  Comes violence geared to the tot.

Comes murder, comes arson, come G-men
  Pursuing unspeakable spies;
Come gangsters and tough-talking he-men
  With six-shooters strapped to their thighs;

Comes the corpse in the dust, comes the dictum
  "Ya' better start singin', ya' rat!"
While the torturer leers at his victim,
  The killer unleashes his gat.

With mayhem the twilight is reeling.
  Blood spatters, the tommy guns bark.
Hands reach for the sky or the ceiling
  As the dagger strikes home in the dark.

And lo! with what rapturous wonder
  The little ones hark to each tale
Of gambler shot down with his plunder
  Or outlaw abducting the mail.

Between the news and the tireless
  Commercials, while tempers turn sour,
Comes a season of horror by wireless,
  That is known as the Children's Hour.
                    —PHYLLIS MCGINLEY (b. 1905)

Places...
Home and Away

"*If you have lived about, you have lost that sense of the absoluteness and the sanctity of the habits of your fellow-patriots which once made you so happy in the midst of them. You have seen that there are a great many patriae in the world, and that each of these is filled with excellent people.*"

—HENRY JAMES

Afro-American Fragment

So long,
So far away
Is Africa.
Not even memories alive
Save those that history books create,
Save those that songs
Beat back into the blood—
Beat out of blood with words sad-sung
In strange un-Negro tongue—
So long,
So far away
Is Africa.

Subdued and time-lost
Are the drums—and yet
Through some vast mist of race
There comes this song
I do not understand,
This song of atavistic land,
Of bitter yearnings lost
Without a place—
So long,
So far away
Is Africa's
Dark face.

—LANGSTON HUGHES (1902–1967)

Home-Thoughts from Abroad

Oh, to be in England
Now that April's there,
And whoever wakes in England
Sees, some morning, unaware,
That the lowest boughs and the brush-wood sheaf
Round the elm-tree bole are in tiny leaf,
While the chaffinch sings on the orchard bough
In England—now!

And after April, when May follows,
And the whitethroat builds, and all the swallows—
Hark! where my blossomed pear-tree in the hedge
Leans to the field and scatters on the clover
Blossoms and dewdrops—at the bent-spray's edge—
That's the wise thrush; he sings each song twice over,
Lest you should think he never could recapture
The first fine careless rapture!
And though the fields look rough with hoary dew,
All will be gay when noontide wakes anew
The buttercups, the little children's dower,
—Far brighter than this gaudy melon-flower!
                    —ROBERT BROWNING (1812–1889)

The Tropics in New York

Bananas ripe and green, the gingerroot,
    Cocoa in pods and alligator pears,
And tangerines and mangoes and grapefruit,
    Fit for the highest prize at parish fairs,

Set in the window, bringing memories
    Of fruit trees laden by low-singing rills,
And dewy dawns, and mystical blue skies
    In benediction over nunlike hills.

My eyes grew dim, and I could no more gaze;
    A wave of longing through my body swept,
And, hungry for the old familiar ways,
    I turned aside and bowed my head and wept.
                    —CLAUDE MCKAY (1890–1948)

That Mountain Far Away

My home over there, my home over there,
My home over there, now I remember it!
And when I see that mountain far away
Why, then I weep. Alas! what can I do?
What can I do? Alas! what can I do?

My home over there, now I remember it.
                            —SONG OF THE TEWA
TRANSLATED BY HERBERT JOSEPH SPINDEN (1879–1967)

I Wonder How My Home Is

In San Juan I wonder how my home is.
Surrounded by green cottonwoods my home is,
Now I remember all and now I sing!
Now I remember how I used to live
And how I used to walk amid my corn
And through my fields. Alas! what can I do?
                            —SONG OF THE TEWA
TRANSLATED BY HERBERT JOSEPH SPINDEN (1879–1967)

London

I wander through each chartered street,
Near where the chartered Thames does flow,
And mark in every face I meet
Marks of weakness, marks of woe.

In every cry of every man,
In every infant's cry of fear,
In every voice, in every ban,
The mind-forged manacles I hear.

How the chimney-sweeper's cry
Every black'ning church appalls;
And the hapless soldier's sigh
Runs in blood down palace walls.

But most through midnight streets I hear
How the youthful harlot's curse
Blasts the new-born infant's tear,
And blights with plagues the marriage hearse.
                            —WILLIAM BLAKE (1757–1827)

Composed upon Westminster Bridge
September 3, 1802

Earth has not anything to show more fair:
Dull would he be of soul who could pass by
A sight so touching in its majesty:
This City now doth, like a garment, wear
The beauty of the morning; silent, bare,
Ships, towers, domes, theaters, and temples lie
Open unto the fields, and to the sky;
All bright and glittering in the smokeless air.
Never did sun more beautifully steep
In his first splendor, valley, rock, or hill;
Ne'er saw I, never felt, a calm so deep!
The river glideth at his own sweet will:
Dear God! the very houses seem asleep;
And all that mighty heart is lying still!
                    —WILLIAM WORDSWORTH (1770–1850)

Cologne

In Köln, a town of monks and bones,[1]
And pavements fang'd with murderous stones
And rags, and hags, and hideous wenches;
I counted two and seventy stenches,
All well defined, and several stinks!
Ye Nymphs that reign o'er sewers and sinks,
The river Rhine, it is well known,
Doth wash your city of Cologne;
But tell me, Nymphs, what power divine
Shall henceforth wash the river Rhine?
                    —SAMUEL TAYLOR COLERIDGE (1772–1834)

---

[1] *Köln:* the German name for Cologne.

Innominatus

Breathes there the man with soul so dead,
Who never to himself hath said,
  "This is my own, my native land!"
Whose heart hath ne'er within him burn'd
As home his footsteps he hath turn'd
  From wandering on a foreign strand?
If such there breathe, go, mark him well;
For him no Minstrel raptures swell;
High though his titles, proud his name,
Boundless his wealth as wish can claim;
Despite those titles, power, and pelf,
The wretch, concentred all in self,
Living, shall forfeit fair renown,
And, doubly dying, shall go down
To the vile dust from whence he sprung,
Unwept, unhonour'd, and unsung.
                —SIR WALTER SCOTT (1771–1832)

Belief

". . . persuasion and belief
Had ripened into faith, and faith became
A passionate intuition."
—WILLIAM WORDSWORTH

The Creation

And God stepped out on space,
And he looked around and said:
I'm lonely—
I'll make me a world.

And far as the eye of God could see
Darkness covered everything,
Blacker than a hundred midnights
Down in a cypress swamp.

Then God smiled,
And the light broke,
And the darkness rolled up on one side,
And the light stood shining on the other,
And God said: That's good!

Then God reached out and took the light in His hands,
And God rolled the light around in His hands
Until He made the sun;
And He set that sun a-blazing in the heavens.
And the light that was left from making the sun
God gathered up in a shining ball
And flung against the darkness,
Spangling the night with the moon and stars.
Then down between
The darkness and the light
He hurled the world;
And God said: That's good!

Then God himself stepped down—
And the sun was on His right hand,
And the moon was on His left;
The stars were clustered about His head,
And the earth was under His feet.
And God walked, and where He trod
His footsteps hollowed the valleys out
And bulged the mountains up.

Then He stopped and looked and saw
That the earth was hot and barren.

So God stepped over to the edge of the world
And He spat out the seven seas—
He batted His eyes, and the lightnings flashed—
He clapped His hands, and the thunders rolled—
And the waters above the earth came down,
The cooling waters came down.

Then the green grass sprouted,
And the little red flowers blossomed,
The pine tree pointed his finger to the sky,
And the oak spread out his arms,
The lakes cuddled down in the hollows of the ground,
And the rivers ran down to the sea;
And God smiled again,
And the rainbow appeared,
And curled itself around His shoulder.

Then God raised His arm and He waved His hand
Over the sea and over the land,
And He said: Bring forth! Bring forth!
And quicker than God could drop His hand,
Fishes and fowls
And beasts and birds
Swam the rivers and the seas,
Roamed the forests and the woods,
And split the air with their wings.
And God said: That's good!

Then God walked around,
And God looked around
On all that He had made.
He looked on His world
With all its living things,
And God said: I'm lonely still.

Then God sat down—
On the side of a hill where He could think;
By a deep, wide river He sat down;
With His head in His hands,
God thought and thought,
Till He thought: I'll make me a man!

Up from the bed of the river
God scooped the clay;

And by the bank of the river
He kneeled Him down;
And there the great God Almighty
Who lit the sun and fixed it in the sky,
Who flung the stars to the most far corner of the night,
Who rounded the earth in the middle of His hand;
This Great God,
Like a mammy bending over her baby,
Kneeled down in the dust
Toiling over a lump of clay
Till He shaped it in His own image;

Then into it He blew the breath of life,
And man became a living soul.
Amen. Amen.

—JAMES WELDON JOHNSON (1871–1938)

Miracles

Why, who makes much of a miracle?
As to me I know of nothing else but miracles,
Whether I walk the streets of Manhattan,
Or dart my sight over the roofs of houses toward the sky,
Or wade with naked feet along the beach just in the edge of
　　the water,
Or stand under trees in the woods,
Or talk by day with any one I love,
Or sit at table at dinner with the rest,
Or look at strangers opposite me riding in the car,
Or watch honey-bees busy around the hive of a summer
　　forenoon,
Or animals feeding in the fields,
Or birds, or the wonderfulness of insects in the air,
Or the wonderfulness of the sundown, or of stars shining so
　　quiet and bright,
Or the exquisite delicate thin curve of the new moon in
　　spring;
These with the rest, one and all are to me miracles,
The whole referring, yet each distinct and in its place.

To me every hour of the light and dark is a miracle,

Every cubic inch of space is a miracle,
Every square yard of the surface of the earth is spread with
    the same,
Every foot of the interior swarms with the same.

To me the sea is a continual miracle,
The fishes that swim—the rocks—the motion of the waves—
    the ships with men in them,
What stranger miracles are there?
                —WALT WHITMAN (1819–1892)

Nothing Will Die

When will the stream be aweary of flowing
      Under my eye?
When will the wind be aweary of blowing
      Over the sky?
When will the clouds be aweary of fleeting?
When will the heart be aweary of beating?
      And nature die?
Never, oh! never, nothing will die;
    The stream flows,
    The wind blows,
    The cloud fleets,
    The heart beats,
      Nothing will die.

Nothing will die;
All things will change
Thro' eternity.
'Tis the world's winter;
Autumn and summer
Are gone long ago;
Earth is dry to the centre,
But spring, a new comer,
A spring rich and strange,
Shall make the winds blow
Round and round,
Thro' and thro',
    Here and there,
    Till the air
And the ground
Shall be fill'd with life anew.

The world was never made;
It will change, but it will not fade.
So let the wind range;
For even and morn
    Ever will be
    Thro' eternity.
Nothing was born;
Nothing will die;
All things will change.
    —ALFRED, LORD TENNYSON (1809–1892)

Psalm 8

O Lord our Lord, how excellent *is* thy name in all the earth!
    who hast set thy glory above the heavens.
Out of the mouth of babes and sucklings hast thou ordained
    strength because of thine enemies, that thou mightest still
    the enemy and the avenger.
When I consider thy heavens, the work of thy fingers, the
    moon and the stars, which thou hast ordained;
What is man, that thou art mindful of him? and the son of
    man, that thou visitest him?
For thou hast made him a little lower than the angels, and
    hast crowned him with glory and honour.
Thou madest him to have dominion over the works of thy
    hands: thou hast put all *things* under his feet:
All sheep and oxen, yea, and the beasts of the field;
The fowl of the air, and the fish of the sea, *and whatsoever*
    passeth through the paths of the seas.
O Lord our Lord, how excellent *is* thy name in all the earth!
    —PSALM OF DAVID 8:1–9

Love

Love bade me welcome; yet my soul drew back,
    Guilty of dust and sin.
But quick-eyed Love, observing me grow slack
    From my first entrance in,

Drew nearer to me, sweetly questioning,
    If I lacked anything.

"A guest," I answered, "worthy to be here."
    Love said, "You shall be he."
"I, the unkind, ungrateful? Ah, my dear,
    I cannot look on Thee!"
Love took my hand and smiling did reply,
    "Who made the eyes but I?"

"Truth, Lord; but I have marred them; let my shame
    Go where it doth deserve."
"And know you not," says Love, "who bore the blame?"
    "My dear, then I will serve."
"You must sit down," says Love, "and taste my meat."
    So I did sit and eat.
                            —GEORGE HERBERT (1593–1633)

Some Keep the Sabbath Going to Church

Some keep the Sabbath going to Church—
I keep it, staying at Home—
With a Bobolink for a Chorister—
And an Orchard, for a Dome—

Some keep the Sabbath in Surplice—
I just wear my Wings
And instead of tolling the Bell for Church,
Our little Sexton—sings.

God preaches, a noted Clergyman—
And the sermon is never long,
So instead of getting to Heaven, at last—
I'm going, all along.
                            —EMILY DICKINSON (1830–1886)

On His Blindness

When I consider how my light is spent
Ere half my days in this dark world and wide,

And that one talent, which is death to hide,
Lodged with me useless, though my soul more bent
To serve therewith my Maker, and present
My true account, lest he returning chide,
"Doth God exact day-labor, light denied?"
I fondly ask. But Patience, to prevent
That murmur, soon replies, "God doth not need
Either man's work or his own gifts; who best
Bear his mild yoke, they serve him best; his state
Is kingly; thousands at his bidding speed,
And post o'er land and ocean without rest;
They also serve who only stand and wait."
—JOHN MILTON (1608–1674)

To Everything There Is a Season

To every *thing there is* a season, and a time to every purpose
under the heaven:
A time to be born, and a time to die; a time to plant, and a
time to pluck up *that which is* planted;
A time to kill, and a time to heal; a time to break down, and
a time to build up;
A time to weep, and a time to laugh; a time to mourn, and
a time to dance;
A time to cast away stones, and a time to gather stones
together; a time to embrace, and a time to refrain from
embracing;
A time to get, and a time to lose; a time to keep, and a time
to cast away;
A time to rend, and a time to sew; a time to keep silence,
and a time to speak;
A time to love, and a time to hate; a time of war, and a time
of peace.

ECCLESIASTES 3:1–8

Nature's Questioning

When I look forth at dawning, pool,
Field, flock, and lonely tree,
All seem to gaze at me
Like chastened children sitting silent in a school;

Their faces dulled, constrained, and worn,
  As though the master's ways
  Through the long teaching days
Had cowed them till their early zest was overborne.

Upon them stirs in lippings mere
  (As if once clear in call,
  But now scarce breathed at all)—
"We wonder, ever wonder, why we find us here!

"Has some Vast Imbecility,
  Might to build and blend,
  But impotent to tend,
Framed us in jest, and left us now to hazardry?

"Or come we of an Automaton
  Unconscious of our pains? . . .
  Or are we live remains
Of Godhead dying downwards, brain and eye now gone?

"Or is that some high Plan betides,
  As yet not understood,
  Of Evil stormed by Good,
We the Forlorn Hope over which Achievement strides?"

Thus things around. No answerer I . . .
  Meanwhile the winds, and rains,
  And Earth's old glooms and pains
Are still the same, and Life and Death are neighbours nigh.
              —THOMAS HARDY (1840–1928)

Design

I found a dimpled spider, fat and white,
On a white heal-all, holding up a moth
Like a white piece of rigid satin cloth—
Assorted characters of death and blight
Mixed ready to begin the morning right,
Like the ingredients of a witches' broth—
A snow-drop spider, a flower like froth,
And dead wings carried like a paper kite.

What had that flower to do with being white,
The wayside blue and innocent heal-all?
What brought the kindred spider to that height,
Then steered the white moth thither in the night?
What but design of darkness to appall?—
If design govern in a thing so small.

      —ROBERT FROST (1874–1963)

Flower in the Crannied Wall

Flower in the crannied wall,
I pluck you out of the crannies,
I hold you here, root and all, in my hand,
Little flower—but *if* I could understand
What you are, root and all, and all in all,
I should know what God and man is.

    —ALFRED, LORD TENNYSON (1809–1892)

My Cathedral

Like two cathedral towers these stately pines
 Uplift their fretted summits tipped with cones;
 The arch beneath them is not built with stones,
 Not Art but Nature traced those lovely lines,
And carved this graceful arabesque of vines;
 No organ but the wind here sighs and moans,
 No sepulchre conceals a martyr's bones,
 No marble bishop on his tomb reclines.
Enter! the pavement, carpeted with leaves,
 Gives back a softened echo to thy tread!
 Listen! the choir is singing; all the birds,
In leafy galleries beneath the eaves,
 Are singing! listen, ere the sound be fled,
 And learn there may be worship without words.

  —HENRY WADSWORTH LONGFELLOW (1807–1882)

"Raise Me Up, Lord" . . .

Raise me up, Lord, who am fallen down,
void of love and fear and faith and awe;
I long to rise and in my place abide;
mine is the longing, mine the impediment.

I am, who am one only, cleft in twain;
I live and die, make merry and lament;
what I can do cannot by me be done;
I flee from evil and tarry in its toils.

I am so hardened in my obduracy
that spite the dread of losing me and thee
I never turn me from my wicked ways.

Between thy might and mercy I am torn;
in others every day I see amend,
in me I see fresh longing to offend thee.
        —MIGUEL DE GUEVARA (1585–1646?)
    TRANSLATED BY SAMUEL BECKETT (b. 1906)

The Preacher: Ruminates behind the Sermon

I think it must be lonely to be God.
Nobody loves a master. No. Despite
The bright hosannas, bright dear-Lords, and bright
Determined reverence of Sunday eyes.

Picture Jehovah striding through the hall
Of His importance, creatures running out
From servant-corners to acclaim, to shout
Appreciation of His merit's glare.

But who walks with Him?—dares to take His arm,
To slap Him on the shoulder, tweak His ear,
Buy Him a Coca-Cola or a beer,
Pooh-pooh His politics, call Him a fool?

Perhaps—who knows?—He tires of looking down.
Those eyes are never lifted. Never straight.
Perhaps sometimes He tires of being great
In solitude. Without a hand to hold.

—GWENDOLYN BROOKS (b. 1917)

Journey of the Magi

"A cold coming we had of it,
Just the worst time of the year
For a journey, and such a long journey:
The ways deep and the weather sharp,
The very dead of winter."
And the camels galled, sore-footed, refractory,
Lying down in the melting snow.
There were times we regretted
The summer palaces on slopes, the terraces,
And the silken girls bringing sherbet.
Then the camel men cursing and grumbling
And running away, and wanting their liquor and
      women,
And the night-fires going out, and the lack of shelters,
And the cities hostile and the towns unfriendly
And the villages dirty and charging high prices:
A hard time we had of it.
At the end we preferred to travel all night,
Sleeping in snatches,
With the voices singing in our ears, saying
That this was all folly.

Then at dawn we came down to a temperate valley,
Wet, below the snow line, smelling of vegetation,
With a running stream and a water-mill beating the
      darkness,
And three trees on the low sky.
And an old white horse galloped away in the meadow.
Then we came to a tavern with vine-leaves over the
      lintel,
Six hands at an open door dicing for pieces of silver,
And feet kicking the empty wine-skins.
But there was no information, and so we continued
And arrived at evening, not a moment too soon

Finding the place; it was (you may say) satisfactory.
All this was a long time ago, I remember,
And I would do it again, but set down
This set down
This: were we led all that way for
Birth or Death? There was a Birth, certainly.
We had evidence and no doubt. I had seen birth and
    death,
But had thought they were different; this Birth was
Hard and bitter agony for us, like Death, our death.
We returned to our places, these Kingdoms,
But no longer at ease here, in the old dispensation,
With an alien people clutching their gods.
I should be glad of another death.

—T. S. ELIOT (1888–1965)

Commitment

*"Find a mission in life and
take it seriously."*
—Dr. William C. Menninger
in answer to the question of how to achieve
mental health (*The New York Times*)

Law Like Love

Law, say the gardeners, is the sun,
Law is the one
All gardeners obey
To-morrow, yesterday, to-day.

Law is the wisdom of the old,
The impotent grandfathers feebly scold;
The grandchildren put out a treble tongue,
Law is the senses of the young.

Law, says the priest with a priestly look,
Expounding to an unpriestly people,
Law is the words in my priestly book,
Law is my pulpit and my steeple.

Law, says the judge as he looks down his nose,
Speaking clearly and most severely,
Law is as I've told you before,
Law is as you know I suppose,
Law is but let me explain it once more,
Law is The Law.

Yet law-abiding scholars write:
Law is neither wrong nor right,
Law is only crimes
Punished by places and by times,
Law is the clothes men wear
Anytime, anywhere,
Law is Good morning and Good night.

Others say, Law is our Fate;
Others say, Law is our State;
Others say, others say
Law is no more,
Law has gone away.

And always the loud angry crowd,
Very angry and very loud,
Law is We,
And always the soft idiot softly Me.

If we, dear, know we know no more
Than they about the Law,
If I no more than you
Know what we should and should not do
Except that all agree
Gladly or miserably
That the Law is
And that all know this,
If therefore thinking it absurd
To identify Law with some other word,
Unlike so many men
I cannot say Law is again,
No more than they can we suppress
The universal wish to guess
Or slip out of our own position
Into an unconcerned condition.
Although I can at least confine
Your vanity and mine
To stating timidly
A timid similarity,
We shall boast anyway:
Like love I say.

Like love we don't know where or why,
Like love we can't compel or fly,
Like love we often weep,
Like love we seldom keep.

—W. H. AUDEN (b. 1907)

Though I Speak with the Tongues of Men and Angels

Though I speak with the tongues of men and of angels, and
    have not love, I am become *as* sounding brass, or a
    tinkling cymbal.
And though I have *the gift of* prophecy, and understand all
    mysteries, and all knowledge; and though I have all
    faith, so that I could remove mountains, and have not
    love, I am nothing.
And though I bestow all my goods to feed *the poor,* and

though I give my body to be burned, and have not love,
it profiteth me nothing.

Love suffereth long, *and* is kind; love envieth not; love
vaunteth not itself, is not puffed up,

Doth not behave itself unseemly, seeketh not her own, is not
easily provoked, thinketh no evil;

Rejoiceth not in iniquity, but rejoiceth in the truth;

Beareth all things, believeth all things, hopeth all things,
endureth all things.

Love never faileth: but whether *there be* prophecies, they
shall fail; whether *there be* tongues, they shall cease;
whether *there be* knowledge, it shall vanish away.

For we know in part, and we prophesy in part.

But when that which is perfect is come, then that which is in
part shall be done away.

When I was a child, I spake as a child, I understood as a
child, I thought as a child: but when I became a man,
I put away childish things.

For now we see through a glass, darkly; but then face to
face: now I know in part; but then shall I know even
as also I am known.

And now abideth faith, hope, love, these three; but the
greatest of these is love.

—CORINTHIANS 13:1–13

I Hear It Was Charged against Me

I hear it was charged against me that I sought to destroy in-
stitutions.

But really I am neither for nor against institutions.

(What indeed have I in common with them? or what with
the destruction of them?)

Only I will establish in the Mannahatta and in every city of
these States inland and seaboard,

And in the fields and woods, and above every keel little or
large that dents the water,

Without edifices or rules or trustees or any argument,

The institution of the dear love of comrades.

—WALT WHITMAN (1819–1892)

I Asked No Other Thing

I asked no other thing,
No other was denied.
I offered Being for it;
The mighty merchant smiled.

Brazil? He twirled a button,
Without a glance my way:
"But, madam, is there nothing else
That we can show to-day?"
                    —EMILY DICKINSON (1830–1886)

Ode on a Grecian Urn

Thou still unravished bride of quietness,
Thou foster-child of silence and slow time,
Sylvan historian, who canst thus express
    A flowery tale more sweetly than our rime:
What leaf-fringed legend haunts about thy shape
    Of deities or mortals, or of both,
        In Tempe or the dales of Arcady?
    What men or gods are these? What maidens loath?
What mad pursuit? What struggle to escape?
        What pipes and timbrels? What wild ecstasy?

Heard melodies are sweet, but those unheard
    Are sweeter; therefore, ye soft pipes, play on;
Not to the sensual ear, but, more endeared,
    Pipe to the spirit ditties of no tone:
Fair youth, beneath the trees, thou canst not leave
    Thy song, nor ever can those trees be bare;
        Bold Lover, never, never canst thou kiss,
Though winning near the goal—yet, do not grieve;
    She cannot fade, though thou hast not thy bliss,
        Forever wilt thou love, and she be fair!

Ah, happy, happy boughs! that cannot shed
    Your leaves, nor ever bid the Spring adieu;
And, happy melodist, unwearièd,

Forever piping songs forever new;
More happy love! more happy, happy love!
　Forever warm and still to be enjoyed,
　　Forever panting, and forever young;
All breathing human passion far above,
　　That leaves a heart high-sorrowful and cloyed,
　　A burning forehead, and a parching tongue.

Who are these coming to the sacrifice?
　　To what green altar, O mysterious priest,
Lead'st thou that heifer lowing at the skies,
　　And all her silken flanks with garlands dressed?
What little town by river or sea shore,
　Or mountain-built with peaceful citadel,
　　Is emptied of this folk, this pious morn?
And, little town, thy streets for evermore
　Will silent be; and not a soul to tell
　　Why thou art desolate, can e'er return.

O Attic shape! Fair attitude! with brede
　Of marble men and maidens overwrought,
With forest branches and the trodden weed;
　Thou, silent form, dost tease us out of thought
As doth eternity: Cold Pastoral!
　When old age shall this generation waste,
　　Thou shalt remain, in midst of other woe
Than ours, a friend to man, to whom thou say'st,
　"Beauty is truth, truth beauty,"—that is all
　　Ye know on earth, and all ye need to know.
　　　　　　　　　—JOHN KEATS (1795–1821)

"My Heart Leaps Up When I Behold"

My heart leaps up when I behold
　A rainbow in the sky:
So was it when my life began;
So is it now I am a man;
So be it when I shall grow old,
　Or let me die!
The Child is father of the Man;

And I could wish my days to be
Bound each to each by natural piety.
—WILLIAM WORDSWORTH (1770–1850)

I Died for Beauty

I died for Beauty—but was scarce
Adjusted in the Tomb
When One who died for Truth, was lain
In an adjoining Room—

He questioned softly "Why I failed"?
"For Beauty", I replied—
"And I—for Truth—Themself are One—
We Brethren, are", He said—

And so, as Kinsmen, met a Night—
We talked between the Rooms—
Until the Moss had reached our lips—
And covered up—our names—
—EMILY DICKINSON (1830–1886)

Sonnet—To Science

Science! true daughter of Old Time thou art!
  Who alterest all things with thy peering eyes.
Why preyest thou thus upon the poet's heart,
  Vulture, whose wings are dull realities?
How should he love thee? or how deem thee wise,
  Who wouldst not leave him in his wandering
To seek for treasure in the jewelled skies,
  Albeit he soared with an undaunted wing?
Hast thou not dragged Diana from her car?
  And driven the Hamadryad from the wood
To seek a shelter in some happier star?
  Hast thou not torn the Naiad from her flood,
The Elfin from the green grass, and from me
The summer dream beneath the tamarind tree?
—EDGAR ALLAN POE (1809–1849)

Solitude

Happy the man whose wish and care
A few paternal acres bound,
Content to breathe his native air
    In his own ground.

Whose herds with milk, whose fields with bread,
Whose flocks supply him with attire;
Whose trees in summer yield him shade,
    In winter fire.

Blest, who can unconcern'dly find
Hours, days, and years slide soft away
In health of body, peace of mind;
    Quiet by day,

Sound sleep by night; study and ease
Together mixed; sweet recreation;
And innocence, which most does please
    With meditation.

Thus let me live, unseen, unknown;
Thus unlamented let me die;
Steal from the world, and not a stone
    Tell where I lie.

        —ALEXANDER POPE (1688–1744

The Old Stone Cross

A statesman is an easy man,
He tells his lies by rote;
A journalist makes up his lies
And takes you by the throat;
So stay at home and drink your beer
And let the neighbours vote,
    Said the man in the golden breastplate
    Under the old stone Cross.

Because this age and the next age
Engender in the ditch,

No man can know a happy man
From any passing wretch;
If Folly link with Elegance
No man knows which is which,
>   *Said the man in the golden breastplate*
>   *Under the old stone Cross.*

But actors lacking music
Do most excite my spleen,
They say it is more human
To shuffle, grunt and groan,
Not knowing what unearthly stuff
Rounds a mighty scene,
>   *Said the man in the golden breastplate*
>   *Under the old stone Cross.*
>   —WILLIAM BUTLER YEATS (1865–1939)

Time, Real and Imaginary
An Allegory

On the wide level of a mountain's head,
(I knew not where, but 'twas some faery place)
Their pinions, ostrich-like, for sails out-spread,
Two lovely children run an endless race,
    A sister and a brother!
    This far outstripp'd the other;
Yet ever runs she with reverted face,
And looks and listens for the boy behind:
    For he, alas! is blind!
O'er rough and smooth with even step he passed,
And knows not whether he be first or last.
        —SAMUEL TAYLOR COLERIDGE (1772–1834)

It Dropped So Low

It dropped so low—in my Regard—
I heard it hit the Ground—
And go to pieces on the Stones
At bottom of my Mind—

Yet blamed the Fate that flung it—*less*
Than I denounced Myself,
For entertaining Plated Wares
Upon my Silver Shelf—
— EMILY DICKINSON (1830–1886)

Magnets

The straight, the swift, the debonair,
Are targets on the thoroughfare
For every kind appraising eye;
Sweet words are said as they pass by.
But such a strange contrary thing
My heart is, it will never cling
To any bright unblemished thing.
Such have their own security,
And little need to lean on me.
The limb that falters in its course,
And cries, "Not yet!" to waning force;
The orb that may not brave the sun;
The bitter mouth, its kissing done;
The loving heart that must deny
The very love it travels by;
What most has need to bend and pray,
These magnets draw my heart their way.
— COUNTEE CULLEN (1903–1946)

The Song of Wandering Aengus

I went out to the hazel wood,
Because a fire was in my head,
And cut and peeled a hazel wand,
And hooked a berry to a thread;
And when white moths were on the wing,
And moth-like stars were flickering out,
I dropped the berry in a stream
And caught a little silver trout.

When I had laid it on the floor
I went to blow the fire aflame,

But something rustled on the floor,
And some one called me by my name:
It had become a glimmering girl
With apple blossom in her hair
Who called me by my name and ran
And faded through the brightening air.

Though I am old with wandering
Through hollow lands and hilly lands,
I will find out where she has gone,
And kiss her lips and take her hands;
And walk among long dappled grass,
And pluck till time and times are done
The silver apples of the moon,
The golden apples of the sun.
　　　　　—WILLIAM BUTLER YEATS (1865–1939)

Nonsense Rhyme

Whatever's good or bad or both
Is surely better than the none;
There's grace in either love or loathe;
Sunlight, or freckles on the sun.

The worst and best are both inclined
To snap like vixens at the truth;
But, O, beware the middle mind
That purrs and never shows a tooth!

Beware the smooth ambiguous smile
That never pulls the lips apart;
Salt of pure and pepper of vile
Must season the extremer heart.

A pinch of fair, a pinch of foul.
And bad and good make best of all;
Beware the moderated soul
That climbs no fractional inch to fall.

Reason's a rabbit in a hutch,
And ecstasy's a were-wolf ghost;

But, O, beware the nothing-much
And welcome madness and the most!
—ELINOR WYLIE (1885–1928)

For Whosoever Will Save His Life Shall Lose It

For whosoever will save his life shall lose it: and whosoever
will lose his life for my sake shall find it.
For what is a man profited, if he shall gain the whole world,
and lose his own soul? Or what shall a man give in
exchange for his own soul?

MATTHEW 16:25–26

Death Is Not Evil, Evil Is Mechanical

Only the human being, absolved from kissing and strife
goes on and on and on, without wandering
fixed upon the hub of the ego
going, yet never wandering, fixed, yet in motion,
the kind of hell that is real, grey and awful
sinless and stainless going round and round
the kind of hell grey Dante never saw
but of which he had a bit inside him.

Know thyself, and that thou art mortal.
But know thyself, denying that thou art mortal:
a thing of kisses and strife
a lit-up shaft of rain
a calling column of blood
a rose tree bronzey with thorns
a mixture of yea and nay
a rainbow of love and hate
a wind that blows back and forth
a creature of beautiful peace, like a river
and a creature of conflict, like a cataract:
know thyself, in denial of all these things—

And thou shalt begin to spin round on the hub of the obscene
ego
a grey void thing that goes without wandering
a machine that in itself is nothing
a centre of the evil world.

D. H. LAWRENCE (1885–1930)

Protest

"We can foresee a time when . . . the only people at liberty will be prison guards who will then have to lock up one another. When only one remains, he will be called the 'Supreme Guard,' and that will be the ideal society in which problems of opposition, the headache of all twentieth century governments, will be settled once and for all."
—ALBERT CAMUS

Song to the Men of England

Men of England, wherefore plow
For the lords who lay ye low?
Wherefore weave with toil and care
The rich robes your tyrants wear?

Wherefore feed, and clothe, and save,
From the cradle to the grave,
Those ungrateful drones who would
Drain your sweat—nay, drink your blood?

Wherefore, bees of England, forge
Many a weapon, chain, and scourge,
That these stingless drones may spoil
The forced produce of your toil?

Have ye leisure, comfort, calm,
Shelter, food, love's gentle balm?
Or what is it ye buy so dear
With your pain and with your fear?

The seed ye sow, another reaps;
The wealth ye find, another keeps;
The robes ye weave, another wears;
The arms ye forge, another bears.

Sow seed—but let no tyrant reap;
Find wealth—let no impostor heap;
Weave robes—let not the idle wear;
Forge arms—in your defense to bear.

Shrink to your cellars, holes, and cells;
In halls ye deck another dwells.
Why shake the chains ye wrought? Ye see
The steel ye tempered glance on ye.

With plow and spade, and hoe and loom,
Trace your grave, and build your tomb,
And weave your winding-sheet, till fair
England be your sepulcher.
—PERCY BYSSHE SHELLEY (1792–1822)

We Shall Overcome

We shall overcome, we shall overcome,
We shall overcome some day, some day;
Oh, deep in my heart, I know that I do believe
We shall overcome some day.

We shall organize, we shall organize,
We shall organize some day, some day;
Oh, deep in my heart, I know that I do believe
We shall organize some day.

We shall end Jim Crow, we shall end Jim Crow,
We shall end Jim Crow some day, some day;
Oh, deep in my heart, I know that I do believe
We shall end Jim Crow some day.

We shall walk in peace, we shall walk in peace,
We shall walk in peace some day, some day;
Oh, deep in my heart, I know that I do believe
We shall walk in peace some day.

We shall build a new world, we shall build a new world,
We shall build a new world some day, some day;
Oh, deep in my heart, I know that I do believe
We shall build a new world some day.

We'll walk hand in hand, we'll walk hand in hand,
We'll walk hand in hand some day, some day;
Oh, deep in my heart, I know that I do believe
We'll walk hand in hand some day.

We shall overcome, we shall overcome,
We shall overcome some day, some day;
Oh, deep in my heart, I know that I do believe
We shall overcome some day.

—COAL MINERS OF WEST VIRGINIA

Get on Board, Little Children

Refrain
  Get on board, little chillen,
  Get on board, little chillen,
  Get on board, little chillen,
  Dere's room for many a mo!

De gospel trains a-comin',
I hear it jus' at han',
I hear de car wheels movin',
An rumblin' thro de lan'.

Refrain

De fare is cheap, an' all can go,
De rich an' poor are dere,
No second class aboard dis train,
No diffrunce in de fare.

Refrain

—NEGRO SPIRITUAL

I Thank God I'm Free at Las'

Refrain
  Free at las'—free at las'—
  I thank God I'm free at las',
  Free at las'—free at las',
  I thank God I'm free at las'.

Way down yonder in de graveyard walk,
I thank God I'm free at las',
Me an' my Jesus gwineter meet an' talk,
I thank God I'm free at las'.

Refrain

On-a my knees when de light pass by,
I thank God I'm free at las',

Tho't my soul would rise and fly,
I thank God I'm free at las'.

Refrain

Some o' dese mornin's, bright an' fair,
I thank God I'm free at las',
Meet my Jesus in de middle of de air,
I thank God I'm free at las'.

Refrain

—NEGRO SPIRITUAL

For My People

For my people everywhere singing their slave songs repeat-
edly: their dirges and their ditties and their blues and
jubilees, praying their prayers nightly to an unknown
god, bending their knees humbly to an unseen power;

For my people lending their strength to the years, to the
gone years and the now years and the maybe years,
washing ironing cooking scrubbing sewing mending hoe-
ing plowing digging planting pruning patching dragging
along never gaining never reaping never knowing and
never understanding;

For my playmates in the clay and dust and sand of Alabama
backyards playing baptizing and preaching and doctor
and jail and soldier and school and mama and cooking
and playhouse and concert and store and hair and Miss
Choomby and company;

For the cramped bewildered years we went to school to
learn the reasons why and the answers to and the people
who and the places where and the days when, in mem-
ory of the bitter hours when we discovered we were
black and poor and small and different and nobody
cared and nobody wondered and nobody understood;

For the boys and girls who grew in spite of these things to
be man and woman, to laugh and dance and sing and

play and drink their wine and religion and success, to marry their playmates and bear children and then die of consumption and anemia and lynching;

For my people thronging 47th Street in Chicago and Lenox Avenue in New York and Rampart Street in New Orleans, lost disinherited dispossessed and happy people filling the cabarets and taverns and other people's pockets needing bread and shoes and milk and land and money and something—something all our own;

For my people walking blindly spreading joy, losing time being lazy, sleeping when hungry, shouting when burdened, drinking when hopeless, tied and shackled and tangled among ourselves by the unseen creatures who tower over us omnisciently and laugh;

For my people blundering and groping and floundering in the dark of churches and schools and clubs and societies, associations and councils and committees and conventions, distressed and disturbed and deceived and devoured by money-hungry glory-craving leeches, preyed on by facile force of state and fad and novelty, by false prophet and holy believer;

For my people standing staring trying to fashion a better way from confusion, from hypocrisy and misunderstanding, trying to fashion a world that will hold all the people, all the faces, all the adams and eves and their countless generations;

Let a new earth rise. Let another world be born. Let a bloody peace be written in the sky. Let a second generation full of courage issue forth; let a people loving freedom come to growth. Let a beauty full of healing and a strength of final clenching be the pulsing in our spirits and our blood. Let the martial songs be written, let the dirges disappear. Let a race of men now rise and take control.

—MARGARET WALKER (b. 1915)

Harlem

What happens to a dream deferred?

> Does it dry up
> like a raisin in the sun?
> Or fester like a sore—
> And then run?
> Does it stink like rotten meat?
> Or crust and sugar over—
> like a syrupy sweet?
>
> Maybe it just sags
> like a heavy load.
>
> *Or does it explode?*
> —LANGSTON HUGHES (1902–1967)

The Last Word

Creep into thy narrow bed,
Creep, and let no more be said!
Vain thy onset! all stands fast;
Thou thyself must break at last.

Let the long contention cease!
Geese are swans, and swans are geese.
Let them have it how they will!
Thou art tired; best be still!

They out-talk'd thee, hiss'd thee, tore thee.
Better men fared thus before thee;
Fired their ringing shot and pass'd,
Hotly charged—and broke at last.

Charge once more, then, and be dumb!
Let the victors, when they come,
When the forts of folly fall,
Find thy body by the wall.
—MATTHEW ARNOLD (1822–1888)

We Wear the Mask

We wear the mask that grins and lies
It hides our cheeks and shades our eyes,—
This debt we pay to human guile;
With torn and bleeding hearts we smile,
And mouth with myriad subtleties.

Why should the world be overwise,
In counting all our tears and sighs?
Nay, let them only see us, while
    We wear the mask.

We smile, but, O great Christ, our cries
To thee from tortured souls arise.
We sing, but oh the clay is vile
Beneath our feet, and long the mile;
But let the world dream otherwise,
    We wear the mask!
                    —PAUL LAURENCE DUNBAR (1872–1906)

The Patriot

An Old Story

I

It was roses, roses, all the way,
    With myrtle mixed in my path like mad:
The house-roofs seemed to heave and sway,
    The church-spires flamed, such flags they had,
A year ago on this very day.

II

The air broke into a mist with bells,
    The old walls rocked with the crowd and cries.
Had I said, "Good folk, mere noise repels—
    "But give me your sun from yonder skies!"
They had answered, "And afterward, what else?"

III

Alack, it was I who leaped at the sun
　　To give it my loving friends to keep!
Nought man could do, have I left undone:
　　And you see my harvest, what I reap
This very day, now a year is run.

IV

There's nobody on the house-tops now—
　　Just a palsied few at the windows set;
For the best of the sight is, all allow,
　　At the Shambles' Gate—or, better yet,
By the very scaffold's foot, I trow.

V

I go in the rain, and, more than needs,
　　A rope cuts both my wrists behind;
And I think, by the feel, my forehead bleeds,
　　For they fling, whoever has a mind,
Stones at me for my year's misdeeds.

VI

Thus I entered, and thus I go!
　　In triumphs, people have dropped down dead.
"Paid by the world, what dost thou owe
　　"Me?"—God might question; now instead,
'T is God shall repay: I am safer so.
　　　　　　　　—ROBERT BROWNING (1812–1889)

Song of the Freedman

We are coming from the cotton fields,
　　We are coming from afar;
We have left the plough, the hoe, the axe,
　　And we are going to war.
We have left the old plantation seat,
　　The sugar and the cane,
Where we worked and toiled with weary feet,
　　In sun and wind and rain.

Chorus
    Then come along my boys,
    O, come, come along,
    Then come along my brothers,
    O come, come along.
    We are coming from the cotton fields,
    We are coming from afar;
    We have left the plough, the hoe, the axe,
    And we are going to war.

We will leave our chains behind us, boys,
    The prison and the rack;
And we'll hide beneath a soldier's coat
    The scars upon our back;
And we'll teach the world a lesson soon,
    If taken by the hand,
How night shall come before 'tis noon
    Upon old Pharaoh's land.

Chorus

                 —CIVIL WAR MARCHING SONG

The White Troops Had Their Orders
But the Negroes Looked Like Men

They had supposed their formula was fixed
They had obeyed instructions to devise
A type of cold, a type of hooded gaze.
But when the Negroes came they were perplexed.
These Negroes looked like men. Besides, it taxed
Time and the temper to remember those
Congenital iniquities that cause
Disfavor of the darkness. Such as boxed
Their feelings properly, complete to tags—
A box for dark men and a box for Other—
Would often find the contents had been scrambled.
Or even switched. Who really gave two figs?
Neither the earth nor heaven ever trembled
And there was nothing startling in the weather.
                 —GWENDOLYN BROOKS (b. 1917)

Color—Caste—Denomination—

Color—Caste—Denomination—
These—are Time's Affair—
Death's diviner Classifying
Does not know they are—

As in sleep—All Hue forgotten—
Tenets—put behind—
Death's large—Democratic fingers
Rub away the Brand—

If Circassian—He is careless—
If He put away
Chrysalis of Blonde—or Umber—
Equal Butterfly—

They emerge from His Obscuring—
What Death—knows so well—
Our minuter intuitions—
Deem unplausible—
                    —EMILY DICKINSON (1830–1886)

Sonnet on Chillon

Eternal Spirit of the chainless Mind!
    Brightest in dungeons, Liberty! thou art,
    For there thy habitation is the heart—
The heart which love of thee alone can bind;
And when thy sons to fetters are consign'd—
    To fetters, and the damp vault's dayless gloom,
    Their country conquers with their martyrdom,
And Freedom's fame finds wings on every wind.
Chillon! thy prison is a holy place,
    And thy sad floor an altar; for 'twas trod,
Until his very steps have left a trace
    Worn, as if thy cold pavement were a sod,
By Bonnivard!—May none those marks efface!
    For they appeal from tyranny to God.
—GEORGE GORDON BYRON, LORD BYRON (1788–1824)

Thought of a Briton on the Subjugation
of Switzerland

Two Voices are there; one is of the sea,
One of the mountains; each a mighty Voice:
In both from age to age thou didst rejoice,
They were thy chosen music, Liberty!
There came a Tyrant, and with holy glee
Thou fought'st against him; but hast vainly striven:
Thou from thy Alpine holds at length art driven,
Where not a torrent murmurs heard by thee.
Of one deep bliss thine ear hath been bereft:
Then cleave, O cleave to that which still is left;
For, high-souled Maid, what sorrow would it be
That mountain floods should thunder as before,
And ocean bellow from his rocky shore,
And neither awful Voice be heard by thee!
—WILLIAM WORDSWORTH (1770–1850)

Much Madness Is Divinest Sense

Much madness is divinest sense
To a discerning eye;
Much sense the starkest madness.
'T is the majority
In this, as all, prevails.
Assent, and you are sane;
Demur,—you're straightway dangerous,
And handled with a chain.
—EMILY DICKINSON (1830–1886)

Yet Do I Marvel

I doubt not God is good, well-meaning, kind,
And did He stoop to quibble could tell why
The little buried mole continues blind,
Why flesh that mirrors Him must some day die,

Make plain the reason tortured Tantalus
Is baited by the fickle fruit, declare
If merely brute caprice dooms Sisyphus
To struggle up a never-ending stair.
Inscrutable His ways are, and immune
To catechism by a mind too strewn
With petty cares to slightly understand
What awful brain compels His awful hand.
Yet do I marvel at this curious thing:
To make a poet black, and bid him sing!

—COUNTEE CULLEN (1903–1946)

War

"War is simply a reversal of civilized life."
—George Orwell

Apostrophe to Man

(on reflecting that the world is ready to go to war again)

Detestable race, continue to expunge yourself, die out.
Breed faster, crowd, encroach, sing hymns, build bombing
    planes;
Make speeches, unveil statues, issue bonds, parade;
Convert again into explosives the bewildered ammonia and
    distracted cellulose;
Convert again into putrescent matter drawing flies
The hopeful bodies of the young, exhort,
Pray, pull long faces, be earnest, be all but overcome, be
    photographed;
Confer, perfect your formulae, commercialize
Bacteria harmful to human tissue,
Put death on the market;
Breed, crowd, encroach, expand, expunge yourself, die out,
Homo called *sapiens.*
          —EDNA ST. VINCENT MILLAY (1892–1950)

The Man He Killed

"Had he and I but met
    By some old ancient inn,
We should have sat us down to wet
    Right many a nipperkin!

"But ranged as infantry,
    And staring face to face,
I shot at him as he at me,
    And killed him in his place.

"I shot him dead because—
    Because he was my foe,
Just so: my foe of course he was;
    That's clear enough; although

"He thought he'd 'list, perhaps
    Off-hand like—just as I—
Was out of work—had sold his traps—
    No other reason why.

"Yes; quaint and curious war is!
   You shoot a fellow down
You'd treat if met where any bar is,
   Or help to half-a-crown."
                    —THOMAS HARDY (1840–1928)

Arms and the Boy

Let the boy try along this bayonet-blade
How cold steel is, and keen with hunger of blood;
Blue with all malice, like a madman's flash;
And thinly drawn with famishing for flesh.

Lend him to stroke these blind, blunt bullet-heads
Which long to nuzzle in the hearts of lads,
Or give him cartridges of fine zinc teeth,
Sharp with the sharpness of grief and death.

For his teeth seem for laughing round an apple.
There lurk no claws behind his fingers supple;
And God will grow no talons at his heels,
Nor antlers through the thickness of his curls.
                    —WILFRED OWEN (1893–1918)

Fare Thee Well

When a Chippewa war party left the village, the women
walked before the warriors, all singing this song. After go-
ing some distance, the women divided and stood in two lines,
between which the warriors passed on their way. The women
then returned to the village still singing the song.

Literal translation: "Come, it is time for you to depart.
We are going on a long journey."

        Fare thee well. The time is come
        For our sad departing,
        We who take the road to war
        Travel on a long journey.

Fare thee well. The warrior's eyes
Must not look beside him;
In departing he must see
Only the camp-fires of the enemy.

Fare thee well. We go to fight
For the tribe's protection,
Yet we know the road to war
Ever is a long journey.

—CHIPPEWA SONG
TRANSLATED BY FRANCES DENSMORE (1867–1957)

The Charge of the Light Brigade

Half a league, half a league,
Half a league, onward,
All in the valley of Death
    Rode the six hundred.
"Forward, the Light Brigade!
Charge for the guns!" he said.
Into the valley of Death
    Rode the six hundred.

"Forward, the Light Brigade!"
Was there a man dismayed?
Not though the soldier knew
    Someone had blundered.
Theirs not to make reply,
Theirs not to reason why,
Theirs but to do and die.
Into the valley of Death
    Rode the six hundred.

Cannon to right of them,
Cannon to left of them,
Cannon in front of them
    Volleyed and thundered;
Stormed at with shot and shell,
Boldly they rode and well,
Into the jaws of Death,
Into the mouth of hell
    Rode the six hundred.

Flashed all their sabers bare,
Flashed as they turned in air
Sabering the gunners there,
Charging an army, while
    All the world wondered.
Plunged in the battery smoke
Right through the line they broke;
Cossack and Russian
Reeled from the saber stroke
    Shattered and sundered,
Then they rode back, but not,
    Not the six hundred.

Cannon to right of them,
Cannon to left of them,
Cannon behind them
    Volleyed and thundered;
Stormed at with shot and shell,
While horse and hero fell,
They that had fought so well
Came through the jaws of Death,
Back from the mouth of hell,
All that was left of them,
    Left of six hundred.

When can their glory fade?
O the wild charge they made!
    All the world wondered.
Honor the charge they made!
Honor the Light Brigade,
    Noble six hundred!
                —ALFRED, LORD TENNYSON (1809–1892)

A Post-Mortem

Searching for souvenirs among some rubble,
A post-atomic-warfare man observed
That "those who made this little bit of trouble
Got only what they asked for and deserved."
    Then, in a kindlier afterthought's release,
    He pitied "them that only asked for peace."
                —SIEGFRIED SASSOON (b. 1886)

The Battle of Blenheim

It was a summer evening;
  Old Kaspar's work was done,
And he before his cottage door
  Was sitting in the sun;
And by him sported on the green
His little grandchild Wilhelmine.

She saw her brother Peterkin
  Roll something large and round,
Which he beside the rivulet
  In playing there had found.
He came to ask what he had found,
That was so large, and smooth, and round.

Old Kaspar took it from the boy,
  Who stood expectant by;
And then the old man shook his head,
  And with a natural sigh,
" 'Tis some poor fellow's skull," said he,
"Who fell in the great victory.

"I find them in the garden,
  For there's many here about;
And often, when I go to plow,
  The plowshare turns them out;
For many thousand men," said he,
"Were slain in that great victory."

"Now tell us what 'twas all about,"
  Young Peterkin, he cries;
And little Wilhelmine looks up
  With wonder-waiting eyes;
"Now tell us all about the war,
And what they fought each other for."

"It was the English," Kaspar cried,
  "Who put the French to rout;
But what they fought each other for,
  I could not well make out;
But everybody said," quoth he,
"That 'twas a famous victory.

"My father lived at Blenheim then,
    Yon little stream hard by;
They burnt his dwelling to the ground,
    And he was forced to fly;
So with his wife and child he fled,
Nor had he where to rest his head.

"With fire and sword the country round
    Was wasted far and wide,
And many a childing mother then,
    And new-born baby, died;
But things like that, you know, must be
At every famous victory.

"They say it was a shocking sight
    After the field was won;
For many thousand bodies here
    Lay rotting in the sun;
But things like that, you know, must be
After a famous victory.

"Great praise the Duke of Marlboro' won,
    And our good Prince Eugene."
"Why, 'twas a very wicked thing!"
    Said little Wilhelmine.
"Nay, nay, my little girl," quoth he;
"It was a famous victory.

"And everybody praised the Duke
    Who this great fight did win."
"But what good came of it at last?"
    Quoth little Peterkin.
"Why, that I cannot tell," said he;
"But 'twas a famous victory."
                    —ROBERT SOUTHEY (1774–1843)

To Lucasta, Going to the Wars

Tell me not, Sweet, I am unkind,
    That from the nunnery
Of thy chaste breast and quiet mind
    To war and arms I fly.

True, a new mistress now I chase,
    The first foe in the field;
And with a stronger faith embrace
    A sword, a horse, a shield.

Yet this inconstancy is such
    As thou too shalt adore;
I could not love thee, Dear, so much,
    Loved I not Honour more.
        —RICHARD LOVELACE (1618–1658)

Ode Written in the Beginning of the Year 1746

How sleep the Brave, who sink to Rest,
By all their Country's Wishes blest!
When *Spring,* with dewy Fingers cold,
Returns to deck their hallow'd Mold,
She there shall dress a sweeter Sod,
Than *Fancy's* Feet have ever trod.

By Fairy Hands their Knell is rung,
By Forms unseen their Dirge is sung;
There *Honour* comes, a Pilgrim grey,
To bless the Turf that wraps their Clay,
And *Freedom* shall a-while repair,
To dwell a weeping Hermit there!
        —WILLIAM COLLINS (1721–1759)

The Hand That Signed the Paper Felled a City

The hand that signed the paper felled a city;
Five sovereign fingers taxed the breath,
Doubled the globe of dead and halved a country;
These five kings did a king to death.

The mighty hand leads to a sloping shoulder,
The finger joints are cramped with chalk;
A goose's quill has put an end to murder
That put an end to talk.

The hand that signed the treaty bred a fever,
And famine grew, and locusts came;
Great is the hand that holds dominion over
Man by a scribbled name.

The five kings count the dead but do not soften
The crusted wound nor pat the brow;
A hand rules pity as a hand rules heaven;
Hands have no tears to flow.

—DYLAN THOMAS (1914–1953)

And He Shall Judge among Nations

And he shall judge among the nations, and shall rebuke
many people: and they shall beat their swords into
plowshares, and their spears into pruninghooks: nation
shall not lift up sword against nation, neither shall they
learn war any more.

—ISAIAH 2:4

Patterns

I walk down the garden paths,
And all the daffodils
Are blowing, and the bright blue squills.
I walk down the patterned garden paths
In my stiff, brocaded gown.
With my powdered hair and jewelled fan,
I too am a rare
Pattern. As I wander down
The garden paths.

My dress is richly figured,
And the train
Makes a pink and silver stain
On the gravel, and the thrift
Of the borders.
Just a plate of current fashion,
Tripping by in high-heeled, ribboned shoes.
Not a softness anywhere about me,
Only whalebone and brocade.
And I sink on a seat in the shade

Of a lime tree. For my passion
Wars against the stiff brocade.
The daffodils and squills
Flutter in the breeze
As they please.
And I weep;
For the lime tree is in blossom
And one small flower has dropped upon my bosom.

And the plashing of waterdrops
In the marble fountain
Comes down the garden paths.
The dripping never stops.
Underneath my stiffened gown
Is the softness of a woman bathing in a marble basin,
A basin in the midst of hedges grown
So thick, she cannot see her lover hiding,
But she guesses he is near,
And the sliding of the water
Seems the stroking of a dear
Hand upon her.
What is Summer in a fine brocaded gown!
I should like to see it lying in a heap upon the ground.
All the pink and silver crumpled up on the ground.

I would be the pink and silver as I ran along the paths,
And he would stumble after,
Bewildered by my laughter.
I should see the sun flashing from his sword-hilt and the
    buckles on his shoes.
I would choose
To lead him in a maze along the patterned paths,
A bright and laughing maze for my heavy-booted lover.
Till he caught me in the shade,
And the buttons of his waistcoat bruised my body as he
    clasped me,
Aching, melting, unafraid.
With the shadows of the leaves and the sundrops,
And the plopping of the waterdrops,
All about us in the open afternoon—
I am very like to swoon
With the weight of this brocade,
For the sun sifts through the shade.

Underneath the fallen blossom
In my bosom,
Is a letter I have hid.
It was brought to me this morning by a rider from the Duke.
"Madam, we regret to inform you that Lord Hartwell
Died in action Thursday se'nnight."
As I read it in the white, morning sunlight,
The letters squirmed like snakes.
"Any answer, Madam," said my footman.
"No," I told him.
"See that the messenger takes some refreshment.
No, no answer."
And I walked into the garden,
Up and down the patterned paths,
In my stiff, correct brocade.
The blue and yellow flowers stood up proudly in the sun,
Each one.
I stood upright too,
Held rigid to the pattern
By the stiffness of my gown.
Up and down I walked,
Up and down.

In a month he would have been my husband.
In a month, here, underneath this lime,
We would have broke the pattern;
He for me, and I for him,
He as Colonel, I as Lady,
On this shady seat.
He had a whim
That sunlight carried blessing.
And I answered, "It shall be as you have said."
Now he is dead.

In Summer and in Winter I shall walk
Up and down
The patterned garden paths
In my stiff, brocaded gown.
The squills and daffodils
Will give place to pillared roses, and to asters, and to snow.
I shall go
Up and down,
In my gown.
Gorgeously arrayed,

Boned and stayed.
And the softnesss of my body will be guarded from embrace
By each button, hook, and lace.
For the man who should loose me is dead,
Fighting with the Duke in Flanders,
In a pattern called a war.
Christ! What are patterns for?

—AMY LOWELL (1874–1925)

Tewa Song of War

Eat, eat, while there is bread,
Drink, drink while there is water;
A day comes when dust shall darken the air
When a blight shall wither the land,
When a cloud shall arise,
When a mountain shall be lifted up,
When a strong man shall seize the city,
When ruin shall fall upon all things,
When the tender leaf shall be destroyed,
When eyes shall be closed in death;
When there shall be three signs on a tree,
Father, son and grandson hanging dead on the same tree;
When the battle flag shall be raised,
And the people scattered abroad in the forest.

—TRANSLATED FROM THE MAYAN
BY DANIEL G. BRINTON (1837–1899)

These

are the desolate, dark weeks
when nature in its barrenness
equals the stupidity of man.

The year plunges into night
and the heart plunges
lower than night

to an empty, windswept place
without sun, stars or moon
but a peculiar light as of thought

that spins a dark fire—
whirling upon itself until,
in the cold, it kindles

to make a man aware of nothing
that he knows, not loneliness
itself—Not a ghost but

would be embraced—emptiness,
despair—(They
whine and whistle) among

the flashes and booms of war;
houses of whose rooms
the cold is greater than can be thought,

the people gone that we loved,
the beds lying empty, the couches
damp, the chairs unused—

Hide it away somewhere
out of the mind, let it get roots
and grow, unrelated to jealous

ears and eyes—for itself.
In this mine they come to dig—all.
Is this the counterfoil to sweetest

music? The source of poetry that
seeing the clock stopped, says,
The clock has stopped

that ticked yesterday so well?
and hears the sound of lakewater
splashing—that is now stone.
—WILLIAM CARLOS WILLIAMS (1883–1963)

The Destruction of Sennacherib

The Assyrian came down like the wolf on the fold,
And his cohorts were gleaming in purple and gold;
And the sheen of their spears was like stars on the sea,
When the blue wave rolls nightly on deep Galilee.

Like the leaves of the forest when summer is green,
That host with their banners at sunset were seen:
Like the leaves of the forest when autumn hath blown,
That host on the morrow laid withered and strown.

For the Angel of Death spread his wings on the blast,
And breathed in the face of the foe as he passed;
And the eyes of the sleepers waxed deadly and chill,
And their hearts but once heaved, and forever grew still!

And there lay the steed with his nostril all wide,
But through it there rolled not the breath of his pride:
And the foam of his gasping lay white on the turf,
And cold as the spray of the rock-beating surf.

And there lay the rider distorted and pale,
With the dew on his brow, and the rust on his mail;
And the tents were all silent, the banners alone,
The lances unlifted, the trumpet unblown.

And the widows of Ashur are loud in their wail,
And the idols are broke in the temple of Baal;
And the might of the Gentile, unsmote by the sword,
Hath melted like snow in the glance of the Lord!

—GEORGE GORDON BYRON, LORD BYRON (1788–1824)

The Conquerors

It seems vainglorious and proud
Of Atom-man to boast aloud
   His prowess homicidal
When one remembers how for years,
With their rude stones and humble spears,
Our sires, at wiping out their peers,
   Were almost never idle.

Despite his under-fissioned art
The Hittite made a splendid start
   Toward smiting lesser nations;
While Tamerlane, it's widely known,
Without a bomb to call his own
   Destroyed whole populations.

Nor did the ancient Persian need
Uranium to kill his Mede,
    The Viking earl, his foeman.
The Greeks got excellent results
With swords and engined catapults.
    A chariot served the Roman.

Mere cannon garnered quite a yield
On Waterloo's tempestuous field.
    At Hastings and at Flodden
Stout countrymen, with just a bow
And arrow, laid their thousands low.
    And Gettysburg was sodden.

Though doubtless now our shrewd machines
Can blow the world to smithereens
    More tidily and so on,
Let's give our ancestors their due.
Their ways were coarse, their weapons few.
But ah! how wondrously they slew
    With what they had to go on.
                    —PHYLLIS McGINLEY (b. 1905)

The Little Girl Saw Her First Troop Parade

The little girl saw her first troop parade and asked, "What
    are those?"
"Soldiers."
"What are soldiers?"
"They are for war. They fight and each tries to kill as many
    of the other side as he can."
The girl held still and studied.
"Do you know . . . I know something?"
"Yes, what is it you know?"
"Sometime they'll give a war and nobody will come."
                    —CARL SANDBURG (1878–1967)

Death

"The end of birth is death; the end of death is birth; this is ordained."
—THE BHAGAVAD-GITA, translated by Sir Edwin Arnold

Death Be Not Proud

Death be not proud, though some have called thee
Mighty and dreadful, for thou art not so;
For those whom thou think'st thou dost overthrow
Die not, poor Death; nor yet canst thou kill me.
From rest and sleep, which but thy pictures be,
Much pleasure, then from thee much more must flow;
And soonest our best men with thee do go,
Rest of their bones and soul's delivery.
Thou'rt slave to fate, chance, kings, and desperate men,
And dost with poison, war, and sickness dwell;
And poppy or charms can make us sleep as well
And better than thy stroke. Why swell'st thou then?
One short sleep past, we wake eternally,
And Death shall be no more; Death, thou shalt die.

—JOHN DONNE (1573–1631)

Last Journey

He has gone
the silent road. He goes
before me. He carries his torch
clear already of the traitorous air.

He goes murmuring the verse he could not say
the last evening.
His smile died and in his eyes
the deep dread trembled of what now he knows.

I call him, follow him. He turns no more
his face to me to say: "father,
here is my youth, I give it up to you,
here is my heart, here is my blood."

When my pursuing steps, by absence quickened,
come up with him,
and we are joined before the burning glass
of time-delivered images,

231

I shall see his face and see his brow
sink on my breast.
There he and I shall know who sets a day
for the departing, and the journey's why.
　　　　　—ENRIQUE GONZALES MARTINEZ (1871–1952)
　　　　　　TRANSLATED BY SAMUEL BECKETT (b. 1906)

Because I Could Not Stop for Death

Because I could not stop for Death,
He kindly stopped for me;
The carriage held but just ourselves
And Immortality.

We slowly drove, he knew no haste,
And I had put away
My labor, and my leisure too,
For his civility.

We passed the school where children played
At wrestling in a ring;
We passed the fields of gazing grain,
We passed the setting sun.

We paused before a house that seemed
A swelling of the ground;
The roof was scarcely visible,
The cornice but a mound.

Since then 'tis centuries; but each
Feels shorter than the day
I first surmised the horses' heads
Were toward eternity.
　　　　　　　　　—EMILY DICKINSON (1830–1886)

Crossing the Bar

Sunset and evening star,
　And one clear call for me!
And may there be no moaning of the bar,
　When I put out to sea,

But such a tide as moving seems asleep,
   Too full for sound and foam,
When that which drew from out the boundless deep
   Turns again home.

Twilight and evening bell,
   And after that the dark!
And may there be no sadness of farewell,
   When I embark;

For tho' from out our bourne of Time and Place
   The flood may bear me far,
I hope to see my Pilot face to face
   When I have crost the bar.
          —ALFRED, LORD TENNYSON (1809–1892)

Fear No More the Heat o' the Sun

From Cymbeline

Fear no more the heat o' the sun,
   Nor the furious winter's rages;
Thou thy worldly task hast done,
   Home art gone, and ta'en thy wages:
Golden lads and girls all must,
As chimney-sweepers, come to dust.

Fear no more the frowns o' the great;
   Thou art past the tyrant's stroke;
Care no more to clothe and eat;
   To thee the reed is as the oak:
The scepter, learning, physic, must
All follow this, and come to dust.

Fear no more the lightning-flash,
   Nor the all-dreaded thunder-stone;
Fear not slander, censure rash;
   Thou hast finished joy and moan:
All lovers young, all lovers must
Consign to thee, and come to dust.

No exorciser harm thee!
   Nor no witchcraft charm thee!
Ghost unlaid forbear thee!
   Nothing ill come near thee!
Quiet consummation have;
And renownèd be thy grave!

—WILLIAM SHAKESPEARE (1564–1616)

Janet Waking

Beautifully Janet slept
Till it was deeply morning. She woke then
And thought about her dainty-feathered hen,
To see how it had kept.

One kiss she gave her mother,
Only a small one gave she to her daddy
Who would have kissed each curl of his shining baby;
No kiss at all for her brother.

"Old Chucky, old Chucky!" she cried,
Running across the world upon the grass
To Chucky's house, and listening. But alas,
Her Chucky had died.

It was a transmogrifying bee
Came droning down on Chucky's old bald head
And sat and put the poison. It scarcely bled,
But how exceedingly

And purply did the knot
Swell with the venom and communicate
Its rigor! Now the poor comb stood up straight
But Chucky did not.

So there was Janet
Kneeling on the wet grass, crying her brown hen
(Translated far beyond the daughters of men)
To rise and walk upon it.

And weeping fast as she had breath
Janet implored us, "Wake her from her sleep!"

And would not be instructed in how deep
Was the forgetful kingdom of death.

—JOHN CROWE RANSOM (b. 1888)

Death the Leveller

The glories of our blood and state
    Are shadows, not substantial things;
There is no armour against fate;
    Death lays his icy hand on kings:
        Sceptre and Crown
        Must tumble down,
And in the dust be equal made
With the poor crooked scythe and spade.

Some men with swords may reap the field,
    And plant fresh laurels where they kill:
But their strong nerves at last must yield;
    They tame but one another still:
        Early or late
        They stoop to fate,
And must give up their murmuring breath
When they, pale captives, creep to death.

The garlands wither on your brow;
    Then boast no more your mighty deeds;
Upon Death's purple altar now
    See where the victor-victim bleeds:
        Your heads must come
        To the cold tomb;
Only the actions of the just
Smell sweet, and blossom in their dust.

—JAMES SHIRLEY (1596–1666)

Elegy Written in a Country Churchyard

The curfew tolls the knell of parting day,
    The lowing herd winds slowly o'er the lea,
The plowman homeward plods his weary way,
    And leaves the world to darkness and to me.

Now fades the glimm'ring landscape on the sight,
    And all the air a solemn stillness holds,
Save where the beetle wheels his droning flight,
    And drowsy tinklings lull the distant folds;

Save that from yonder ivy-mantled tow'r
    The moping owl does to the moon complain
Of such, as wand'ring near her secret bow'r,
    Molest her ancient solitary reign.

Beneath those rugged elms, that yew-tree's shade,
    Where heaves the turf in many a mold'ring heap,
Each in his narrow cell forever laid,
    The rude forefathers of the hamlet sleep.

The breezy call of incense-breathing Morn,
    The swallow twitt'ring from the straw-built shed,
The cock's shrill clarion, or the echoing horn,
    No more shall rouse them from their lowly bed.

For them no more the blazing hearth shall burn,
    Or busy housewife ply her evening care;
No children run to lisp their sire's return,
    Or climb his knees the envied kiss to share.

Oft did the harvest to their sickle yield,
    Their furrow oft the stubborn glebe has broke;
How jocund did they drive their team afield!
    How bowed the woods beneath their sturdy stroke!

Let not Ambition mock their useful toil,
    Their homely joys, and destiny obscure;
Nor Grandeur hear with a disdainful smile,
    The short and simple annals of the poor.

The boast of heraldry, the pomp of pow'r,
    And all that beauty, all that wealth e'er gave,
Awaits alike the inevitable hour:
    The paths of glory lead but to the grave.

Nor you, ye proud, impute to these the fault,
    If Mem'ry o'er their tomb no trophies raise,
Where through the long-drawn aisle and fretted vault
    The pealing anthem swells the note of praise.

Can storied urn or animated bust
   Back to its mansion call the fleeting breath?
Can Honor's voice provoke the silent dust,
   Or Flatt'ry soothe the dull cold ear of Death?

Perhaps in this neglected spot is laid
   Some heart once pregnant with celestial fire;
Hands that the rod of empire might have swayed,
   Or waked to ecstasy the living lyre.

But Knowledge to their eyes her ample page
   Rich with the spoils of time did ne'er unroll;
Chill Penury repressed their noble rage,
   And froze the genial current of the soul.

Full many a gem of purest ray serene,
   The dark unfathomed caves of ocean bear;
Full many a flower is born to blush unseen,
   And waste its sweetness on the desert air.

Some village Hampden, that with dauntless breast
   The little tyrant of his fields withstood;
Some mute inglorious Milton here may rest,
   Some Cromwell guiltless of his country's blood.

Th' applause of listening senates to command,
   The threats of pain and ruin to despise,
To scatter plenty o'er a smiling land,
   And read their hist'ry in a nation's eyes,

Their lot forbade; nor circumscribed alone
   Their growing virtues, but their crimes confined;
Forbade to wade through slaughter to a throne,
   And shut the gates of mercy on mankind,

The struggling pangs of conscious truth to hide,
   To quench the blushes of ingenuous shame,
Or heap the shrine of Luxury and Pride
   With incense kindled at the Muse's flame.

Far from the madding crowd's ignoble strife,
   Their sober wishes never learned to stray;
Along the cool sequestered vale of life
   They kept the noiseless tenor of their way.

Yet ev'n these bones from insult to protect
   Some frail memorial still erected nigh,
With uncouth rimes and shapeless sculpture decked,
   Implores the passing tribute of a sigh.

Their name, their years, spelt by th' unlettered Muse,
   The place of fame and elegy supply;
And many a holy text around she strews,
   That teach the rustic moralist to die.

For who, to dumb Forgetfulness a prey,
   This pleasing anxious being e'er resigned,
Left the warm precincts of the cheerful day,
   Nor cast one longing ling'ring look behind?

On some fond breast the parting soul relies,
   Some pious drops the closing eye requires;
Ev'n from the tomb the voice of Nature cries,
   Ev'n in our ashes live their wonted fires.

For thee, who mindful of th' unhonored dead
   Dost in these lines their artless tale relate;
If chance, by lonely Contemplation led,
   Some kindred spirit shall inquire thy fate,

Haply some hoary-headed swain may say,
   "Oft have we seen him at the peep of dawn
Brushing with hasty steps the dews away
   To meet the sun upon the upland lawn.

"There at the foot of yonder nodding beech
   That wreathes its old fantastic roots so high,
His listless length at noontide would he stretch,
   And pore upon the brook that babbles by.

"Hard by yon wood, now smiling as in scorn,
   Mutt'ring his wayward fancies he would rove,
Now drooping, woeful wan, like one forlorn,
   Or crazed with care, or crossed in hopeless love.

"One morn I missed him on the customed hill,
   Along the heath and near his fav'rite tree;
Another came; nor yet beside the rill,
   Nor up the lawn, nor at the wood was he;

"The next with dirges due in sad array
  Slow through the church-way path we saw him borne.
Approach and read (for thou canst read) the lay,
  Graved on the stone beneath yon aged thorn."

THE EPITAPH

Here rests his head upon the lap of Earth
  A Youth to Fortune and to Fame unknown.
Fair Science frowned not on his humble birth,
  And Melancholy marked him for her own.
                    —THOMAS GRAY (1716-1771)

When I Am Dead, My Dearest

When I am dead, my dearest,
  Sing no sad songs for me;
Plant thou no roses at my head,
  Nor shady cypress tree:
Be the green grass above me
  With showers and dewdrops wet;
And if thou wilt, remember,
  And if thou wilt, forget.

I shall not see the shadows,
  I shall not feel the rain;
I shall not hear the nightingale
  Sing on, as if in pain;
And dreaming through the twilight
  That doth not rise nor set,
Haply I may remember,
  And haply may forget.
                    —CHRISTINA ROSSETTI (1830–1894)

The Woodspurge

The wind flapped loose, the wind was still,
Shaken out dead from tree and hill;
I had walked on at the wind's will—
I sat now, for the wind was still.

Between my knees my forehead was—
My lips, drawn in, said not Alas!
My hair was over in the grass,
My naked ears heard the day pass.

My eyes, wide open, had the run
Of some ten weeds to fix upon;
Among these few, out of the sun,
The woodspurge flowered, three cups in one.

From perfect grief there need not be
Wisdom or even memory;
One thing then learned remains to me—
The woodspurge has a cup of three.
                    —DANTE GABRIEL ROSSETTI (1828–1882)

Interlude

Writing, I crushed an insect with my nail
And thought nothing at all. A bit of wing
Caught my eye then, a gossamer so frail

And exquisite, I saw in it a thing
That scorned the grossness of the thing I wrote.
It hung upon my finger like a sting.

A leg I noticed next, fine as a mote,
"And on this frail eyelash he walked," I said,
"And climbed and walked like any mountain-goat."

And in this mood I sought the little head,
But it was lost; then in my heart a fear
Cried out, "A life—why beautiful, why dead!"

It was a mite that held itself most dear,
So small I could have drowned it with a tear.
                    —KARL SHAPIRO (b. 1913)

To an Athlete Dying Young

The time you won your town the race
We chaired you through the market-place;
Man and boy stood cheering by,
And home we brought you shoulder-high.

To-day, the road all runners come,
Shoulder-high we bring you home,
And set you at your threshold down,
Townsman of a stiller town.

Smart lad, to slip betimes away
From fields where glory does not stay
And early though the laurel grows
It withers quicker than the rose.

Eyes the shady night has shut
Cannot see the record cut,
And silence sounds no worse than cheers
After earth has stopped the ears:

Now you will not swell the rout
Of lads that wore their honors out,
Runners whom renown outran
And the name died before the man.

So set, before its echoes fade,
The fleet foot on the sill of shade,
And hold to the low lintel up
The still-defended challenge-cup.

And round that early-laurelled head
Will flock to gaze the strengthless dead,
And find unwithered on its curls
The garland briefer than a girl's.
—A. E. HOUSMAN (1859–1936)

Stanzas

I heard thy fate without a tear,
　　Thy loss with scarce a sigh;
And yet thou wert surpassing dear—
　　Too loved of all to die.

I know not what hath sear'd mine eye:
　　The tears refuse to start;
But every drop its lids deny
　　Falls dreary on my heart.

Yes—deep and heavy, one by one,
　　They sink, and turn to care;
As cavern'd waters wear the stone,
　　Yet, dropping, harden there.

They cannot petrify more fast
　　Than feelings sunk remain,
Which, coldly fix'd, regard the past,
　　But never melt again.
—GEORGE GORDON BYRON, LORD BYRON (1788–1824)

Requiescat

Strew on her roses, roses,
　　And never a spray of yew.
In quiet she reposes:
　　Ah! would that I did too.

Her mirth the world required:
　　She bath'd it in smiles of glee.
But her heart was tired, tired,
　　And now they let her be.

Her life was turning, turning,
　　In mazes of heat and sound.
But for peace her soul was yearning,
　　And now peace laps her round.

Her cabin'd, ample Spirit,
    It flutter'd and fail'd for breath.
To-night it doth inherit
    The vasty Hall of Death.
                    —MATTHEW ARNOLD (1822–1888)

To Die Takes Just a Little While

To die—takes just a little while—
They say it doesn't hurt—
It's only fainter—by degrees—
And then—it's out of sight—

A darker Ribbon—for a Day—
A Crape upon the Hat—
And then the pretty sunshine comes—
And helps us to forget—

The absent—mystic—creature—
That but for love of us—
Had gone to sleep—that soundest time—
Without the weariness—
                    —EMILY DICKINSON (1830–1886)

A Slumber Did My Spirit Seal

A slumber did my spirit seal;
    I had no human fears:
She seem'd a thing that could not feel
    The touch of earthly years.

No motion has she now, no force;
    She neither hears nor sees;
Roll'd round in earth's diurnal course,
    With rocks, and stones, and trees.
                    —WILLIAM WORDSWORTH (1770–1850)

The Force That through the Green Fuse
Drives the Flower

The force that through the green fuse drives the flower
Drives my green age; that blasts the roots of trees
Is my destroyer.
And I am dumb to tell the crooked rose
My youth is bent by the same wintry fever.

The force that drives the water through the rocks
Drives my red blood; that dries the mouthing streams
Turns mine to wax.
And I am dumb to mouth unto my veins
How at the mountain spring the same mouth sucks.

The hand that whirls the water in the pool
Stirs the quicksand; that ropes the blowing wind
Hauls my shroud sail.
And I am dumb to tell the hanging man
How of my clay is made the hangman's lime.

The lips of time leech to the fountain head;
Love drips and gathers, but the fallen blood
Shall calm her sores.
And I am dumb to tell a weather's wind
How time has ticked a heaven round the stars.

And I am dumb to tell the lover's tomb
How at my sheet goes the same crooked worm.

—DYLAN THOMAS (1914–1953)

Alienation

"The experience of separateness arouses anxiety; it is, indeed, the source of all anxiety. Being separate means being cut off without any capacity to use my human powers . . . it means that the world may invade me without my ability to react."
—ERICH FROMM

Useless Words

So long as we speak the same language and never understand
    each other,
So long as the spirals of our words snarl and interlock
And clutch each other with the irreckonable gutturals,
Well . . .

             —CARL SANDBURG (1878–1967)

Written in Northampton County Asylum

I am! yet what I am who cares, or knows?
   My friends forsake me like a memory lost.
I am the self-consumer of my woes;
   They rise and vanish, an oblivious host,
Shadows of life, whose very soul is lost.
And yet I am—I live—though I am toss'd

Into the nothingness of scorn and noise,
   Into the living sea of waking dream,
Where there is neither sense of life, nor joys,
   But the huge shipwreck of my own esteem
And all that's dear. Even those I loved the best
Are strange—nay, they are stranger than the rest.

I long for scenes where man has never trod—
   For scenes where woman never smiled or wept—
There to abide with my Creator, God,
   And sleep as I in childhood sweetly slept,
Full of high thoughts, unborn. So let me die,—
The grass below; above, the vaulted sky.

             —JOHN CLARE (1793–1864)

ALONE/december/night

it's been so long
speaking to people

247

who think it all
too complex
stupidity in their eyes
&
it's been so long
so far from the truth
so far from a roof
to talk to
or a hand to touch
or anything to really
love

it's been so long
talking to myself
alone
in the night
listening to a music
that is me.

—VICTOR CRUZ (b. 1949)

A Noiseless Patient Spider

A noiseless patient spider,
I mark'd where on a little promontory it stood isolated,
Mark'd how to explore the vacant vast surrounding,
It launched forth filament, filament, filament, out of itself,
Ever unreeling them, ever tirelessly speeding them.
And you O my soul where you stand,
Surrounded, detached, in measureless oceans of space,
Ceaselessly musing, venturing, throwing, seeking the spheres
    to connect them,
Till the bridge you will need be form'd, till the ductile anchor
    hold,
Till the gossamer thread you fling catch somewhere, O my
    soul.

—WALT WHITMAN (1819–1892)

Self-Dependence

Weary of myself, and sick of asking
What I am, and what I ought to be,
At this vessel's prow I stand, which bears me
Forwards, forwards, o'er the starlit sea.

And a look of passionate desire
O'er the sea and to the stars I send:
"Ye who from my childhood up have calmed me,
Calm me, ah, compose me to the end!

"Ah, once more," I cried, "ye stars, ye waters,
On my heart your mighty charm renew;
Still, still let me, as I gaze upon you,
Feel my soul becoming vast like you!"

From the intense, clear, star-sown vault of heaven,
Over the lit sea's unquiet way,
In the rustling night-air came the answer:
"Wouldst thou *be* as these are? *Live* as they.

"Unaffrighted by the silence round them,
Undistracted by the sights they see,
These demand not that the things without them
Yield them love, amusement, sympathy.

"And with joy the stars perform their shining,
And the sea its long moon-silvered roll;
For self-poised they live, nor pine with noting
All the fever of some differing soul.

"Bounded by themselves, and unregardful
In what state God's other works may be,
In their own tasks all their powers pouring,
These attain the mighty life you see."

O air-born voice! long since, severely clear,
A cry like thine in mine own heart I hear:
"Resolve to be thyself; and know that he
Who finds himself loses his misery!"
                        —MATTHEW ARNOLD (1822–1888)

In a Dark Time

In a dark time, the eye begins to see,
I meet my shadow in the deepening shade;
I hear my echo in the echoing wood—
A lord of nature weeping to a tree.
I live between the heron and the wren,
Beasts of the hill and serpents of the den.

What's madness but nobility of soul
At odds with circumstance? The day's on fire!
I know the purity of pure despair,
My shadow pinned against a sweating wall.
That place among the rocks—is it a cave,
Or winding path? The edge is what I have.

A steady storm of correspondences!
A night flowing with birds, a ragged moon,
And in broad day the midnight come again!
A man goes far to find out what he is—
Death of the self in a long, tearless night,
All natural shapes blazing unnatural light.

Dark, dark my light, and darker my desire.
My soul, like some heat-maddened summer fly,
Keeps buzzing at the sill. Which I is *I*?
A fallen man, I climb out of my fear.
The mind enters itself, and God the mind,
And one is One, free in the tearing wind.

—THEODORE ROETHKE (1908–1963)

The World Is Too Much with Us; Late and Soon

The world is too much with us; late and soon,
Getting and spending, we lay waste our powers;
Little we see in Nature that is ours;
We have given our hearts away, a sordid boon!
This Sea that bares her bosom to the moon!
The winds that will be howling at all hours,
And are up-gathered now like sleeping flowers;

For this, for everything, we are out of tune;
It moves us not—Great God! I'd rather be
A Pagan suckled in a creed outworn;
So might I, standing on this pleasant lea,
Have glimpses that would make me less forlorn;
Have sight of Proteus rising from the sea;
Or hear old Triton blow his wreathèd horn.
                —WILLIAM WORDSWORTH (1770–1850)

Stanzas Written in Dejection Near Naples

I

The sun is warm, the sky is clear,
    The waves are dancing fast and bright,
Blue isles and snowy mountains wear
    The purple noon's transparent might,
    The breath of the moist earth is light,
Around its unexpanded buds;
    Like many a voice of one delight,
The winds, the birds, the ocean floods,
The City's voice itself, is soft like Solitude's.

II

I see the Deep's untrampled floor
    With green and purple seaweeds strown;
I see the waves upon the shore,
    Like light dissolved in star-showers, thrown:
    I sit upon the sands alone,—
The lightning of the noontide ocean
    Is flashing round me, and a tone
Arises from its measured motion,
How sweet! did any heart now share in my emotion.

III

Alas! I have nor hope nor health,
    Nor peace within nor calm around,
Nor that content surpassing wealth
    The sage in meditation found,
    And walked with inward glory crowned—
Nor fame, nor power, nor love, nor leisure.

Others I see whom these surround—
Smiling they live, and call life pleasure;—
To me that cup has been dealt in another measure.

IV

Yet now despair itself is mild,
    Even as the winds and waters are;
I could lie down like a tired child,
    And weep away the life of care
    Which I have borne and yet must bear,
Till death like sleep might steal on me,
    And I might feel in the warm air
My cheek grow cold, and hear the sea
Breathe o'er my dying brain its last monotony.

V

Some might lament that I were cold,
    As I, when this sweet day is gone,
Which my lost heart, too soon grown old,
    Insults with this untimely moan;
    They might lament—for I am one
Whom men love not,—and yet regret,
    Unlike this day, which, when the sun
Shall on its stainless glory set,
Will linger, though enjoyed, like joy in memory yet.
                    —PERCY BYSSHE SHELLEY (1792–1822)

The Invention of Comics

I am a soul in the world: in
the world of my soul the whirled
light / from the day
the sacked land
of my father.

In the world, the sad
nature of
myself. In myself
nature is sad. Small
prints of the day. Its
small dull fires. Its
sun, like a greyness
smeared on the dark.

The day of my soul, is
the nature of that
place. It is a landscape. Seen
from the top of a hill. A
grey expanse; dull fires
throbbing on its seas.

The man's soul, the complexion
of his life. The menace
of its greyness. The
fire, throbs, the sea
moves. Birds shoot
from the dark. The edge
of the waters lit
darkly for the moon.

And the moon, from the soul. Is
the world, of the man. The man
and his sea, and its moon, and
the soft fire throbbing. Kind
death. O,
my dark and sultry
love.

      —LeRoi Jones (b. 1934)

Psyche

The butterfly the ancient Grecians made
The soul's fair emblem, and its only name—
But of the soul, escaped the slavish trade
Of mortal life!—For in this earthly frame
Ours is a reptile's lot, much toil, much blame,
Manifold motions making little speed,
And to deform and kill the things on which we feed.
    —Samuel Taylor Coleridge (1772–1834)

The Sound of Silence

Hello darkness my old friend,
I've come to talk with you again,
Because a vision softly creeping,
Left its seeds while I was sleeping
And the vision that was planted in my brain
Still remains within the sound of silence.

In restless dreams I walked alone,
Narrow streets of cobble stone
'Neath the halo of a street lamp,
I turned my collar to the cold and damp
When my eyes were stabbed by the flash of a neon light
That split the night, and touched the sound of silence.

And in the naked light I saw
Ten thousand people maybe more,
People talking without speaking,
People hearing without listening,
People writing songs that voices never share
And no one dares disturb the sound of silence.

"Fools!" said I, "You do not know
Silence like a cancer grows.
Hear my words that I might teach you
Take my arms that I might reach you."
But my words like silent raindrops fell
And echoed, in the wells of silence.

And the people bowed and prayed
To the neon God they made,
And the sign flashed out its warning
In the words that it was forming.
And the sign said:
    "The words of the prophets are written
    on the subway walls and tenement halls"
And whispered in the sounds of silence.

—PAUL SIMON (b. 1941)
(SIMON AND GARFUNKEL)

Human Condition

"It was the best of times, it was the worst of times, it was the age of wisdom, it was the age of foolishness, it was the epoch of belief, it was the epoch of incredulity, it was the season of Light, it was the season of Darkness, it was the spring of hope, it was the winter of despair."
—CHARLES DICKENS

The Second Coming

Turning and turning in the widening gyre
The falcon cannot hear the falconer;
Things fall apart; the centre cannot hold;
Mere anarchy is loosed upon the world,
The blood-dimmed tide is loosed, and everywhere
The ceremony of innocence is drowned;
The best lack all conviction, while the worst
Are full of passionate intensity.

Surely some revelation is at hand;
Surely the Second Coming is at hand.
The Second Coming! Hardly are those words out
When a vast image out of *Spiritus Mundi*
Troubles my sight: somewhere in sands of the desert
A shape with lion body and the head of a man,
A gaze blank and pitiless as the sun,
Is moving its slow thighs, while all about it
Reel shadows of the indignant desert birds.
The darkness drops again; but now I know
That twenty centuries of stony sleep
Were vexed to nightmare by a rocking cradle,
And what rough beast, its hour come round at last,
Slouches towards Bethlehem to be born?
                    —WILLIAM BUTLER YEATS (1865–1939)

Prayer before Birth

I am not yet born; O hear me.
Let the bloodsucking bat or the rat or the stoat or the
    club-footed ghoul come near me.

I am not yet born; console me.
I fear that the human race may with tall walls wall me,
    with strong drugs dope me, with wise lies lure me,
        on black racks rack me, in blood-baths roll me.

I am not yet born; provide me
With water to dandle me, grass to grow for me, trees to talk
   to me, sky to sing to me, birds and a white light
     in the back of my mind to guide me.

I am not yet born; forgive me
For the sins that in me the world shall commit, my words
   when they speak me, my thoughts when they think me,
     my treason engendered by traitors beyond me,
       my life when they murder by means of my
        hands, my death when they live me.

I am not yet born; rehearse me
In the parts I must play and the cues I must take when
   old men lecture me, bureaucrats hector me, mountains
     frown at me, lovers laugh at me, the white
       waves call me to folly and the desert calls
        me to doom and the beggar refuses
         my gift and my children curse me.

I am not yet born; O hear me,
Let not the man who is beast or who thinks he is God
   come near me.

I am not yet born; O fill me
With strength against those who would freeze my
   humanity, would dragoon me into a lethal automaton,
     would make me a cog in a machine, a thing with
       one face, a thing, and against all those
        who would dissipate my entirety, would
         blow me like thistledown hither and
          thither or hither and thither
           like water held in the
            hands would spill me.

Let them not make me a stone and let them not spill me.
   Otherwise kill me.

               —LOUIS MACNEICE (1907–1963)

The End of the World

Quite unexpectedly as Vasserot
The armless ambidextrian was lighting

A match between his great and second toe
And Ralph the lion was engaged in biting
The neck of Mme. Sossman while the drum
Pointed, and Teeny was about to cough
In waltz-time swinging Jocko by the thumb—
Quite unexpectedly the top blew off:

And there, there overhead, there, there, hung over
Those thousands of white faces, those dazed eyes,
There in the starless dark, the poise, the hover,
There with vast wings across the canceled skies,
There in the sudden blackness, the black pall
Of nothing, nothing, nothing—nothing at all.

—ARCHIBALD MACLEISH (b. 1892)

Lack of Steadfastness

Sometime this world was so steadfast and stable,
That a man's word was his obligation,
And now it is so false and deceiving
That word and deed are, in conclusion,
No such thing; for turned so upside down
Is all this world for profit and wilfulness
That all is lost for lack of steadfastness.

What makes this world to be so variable,
But that folks lust for dissension?
Among us now a man is thought lacking in ability
Unless he can, by some collusion,
Do to his neighbor wrong or oppression.
What causes this but wilful wickedness
That all is lost for lack of steadfastness.

The truth is put down, reason is held a fable,
Virtue hath now no domination,
Pity is exiled, no man is merciful.
Through covetousness is blent discretion;
The world has made a transformation
From right to wrong, from truth to fickleness,
That all is lost, for lack of steadfastness.

Envoi to King Richard

O prince, strive always to be honorable,
Cherish thy people and hate extortion;
Suffer nothing that may be reprehensible
To thine estate, done in thy realm.
Show forth thy sword of castigation,
Fear God, obey the law, love truth and worthiness,
And wed your people again to steadfastness.

                    —GEOFFREY CHAUCER (c. 1340–1400)

The Hollow Men

Mistah Kurtz—he dead.

                    A penny for the Old Guy

I

We are the hollow men
We are the stuffed men
Leaning together
Headpiece filled with straw. Alas!
Our dried voices, when
We whisper together
Are quiet and meaningless
As wind in dry grass
Or rats' feet over broken glass
In our dry cellar

Shape without form, shade without colour,
Paralysed force, gesture without motion;

Those who have crossed
With direct eyes, to death's other Kingdom
Remember us—if at all—not as lost
Violent souls, but only
As the hollow men
The stuffed men.

II

Eyes I dare not meet in dreams
In death's dream kingdom

These do not appear:
There, the eyes are
Sunlight on a broken column
There, is a tree swinging
And voices are
In the wind's singing
More distant and more solemn
Than a fading star.

Let me be no nearer
In death's dream kingdom
Let me also wear
Such deliberate disguises
Rat's coat, crowskin, crossed staves
In a field
Behaving as the wind behaves
No nearer—

Not that final meeting
In the twilight kingdom

III

This is the dead land
This is cactus land
Here the stone images
Are raised, here they receive
The supplication of a dead man's hand
Under the twinkle of a fading star.

Is it like this
In death's other kingdom
Waking alone
At the hour when we are
Trembling with tenderness
Lips that would kiss
Form prayers to broken stone.

IV

The eyes are not here
There are no eyes here
In this valley of dying stars
In this hollow valley
This broken jaw of our lost kingdoms

In this last of meeting places
We grope together
And avoid speech
Gathered on this beach of the tumid river

Sightless, unless
The eyes reappear
As the perpetual star
Multifoliate rose
Of death's twilight kingdom
The hope only
Of empty men.

V

Here we go round the prickly pear
Prickly pear prickly pear
Here we go round the prickly pear
At five o'clock in the morning.

Between the idea
And the reality
Between the motion
And the act
Falls the Shadow

For Thine is the Kingdom

Between the conception
And the creation
Between the emotion
And the response
Falls the Shadow

Life is very long

Between the desire
And the spasm
Between the potency
And the existence
Between the essence
And the descent
Falls the Shadow

For Thine is the Kingdom

For Thine is
Life is
For Thine is the

This is the way the world ends
This is the way the world ends
This is the way the world ends
Not with a bang but a whimper.
                    —T. S. ELIOT (1888–1965)

England in 1819

An old, mad, blind, despised, and dying king,—
Princes, the dregs of their dull race, who flow
Through public scorn,—mud from a muddy spring,—
Rulers who neither see, nor feel, nor know,
But leech-like to their fainting country cling,
Till they drop, blind in blood, without a blow,—
A people starved and stabbed in the untilled field,—
An army, which liberticide and prey
Makes as a two-edged sword to all who wield,—
Golden and sanguine laws which tempt and slay;
Religion Christless, Godless—a book sealed;
A Senate,—Time's worst statute unrepealed,—
Are graves, from which a glorious Phantom may
Burst, to illumine our tempestuous day.
                —PERCY BYSSHE SHELLEY (1792–1822)

As I Walked Out One Evening

As I walked out one evening,
    Walking down Bristol Street,
The crowds upon the pavement
    Were fields of harvest wheat.

And down by the brimming river
    I heard a lover sing
Under an arch of the railway:
    "Love has no ending.

"I'll love you, dear, I'll love you
    Till China and Africa meet,
And the river jumps over the mountain
    And the salmon sing in the street,

"I'll love you till the ocean
   Is folded and hung up to dry
And the seven stars go squawking
   Like geese about the sky.

"The years shall run like rabbits,
   For in my arms I hold
The Flower of the Ages,
   And the first love of the world."

But all the clocks in the city
   Began to whirr and chime:
"O let not Time deceive you,
   You cannot conquer Time.

"In the burrows of the Nightmare
   Where Justice naked is,
Time watches from the shadow
   And coughs when you would kiss.

"In headaches and in worry
   Vaguely life leaks away,
And Time will have his fancy
   To-morrow or to-day.

"Into many a green valley
   Drifts the appalling snow;
Time breaks the threaded dances
   And the diver's brilliant bow.

"O plunge your hands in water,
   Plunge them in up to the wrist;
Stare, stare in the basin
   And wonder what you've missed.

"The glacier knocks in the cupboard,
   The desert sighs in the bed,
And the crack in the tea-cup opens
   A lane to the land of the dead.

"Where the beggars raffle the banknotes
   And the Giant is enchanting to Jack,
And the Lily-white Boy is a Roarer,
   And Jill goes down on her back.

"O look, look in the mirror,
    O look in your distress;
Life remains a blessing
    Although you cannot bless.

"O stand, stand at the window
    As the tears scald and sta t;
You shall love your crooked neighbour
    With your crooked heart."

It was late, late in the evening,
    The lovers they were gone;
The clocks had ceased their chiming,
    And the deep river ran on.
                                    —W. H. AUDEN (b. 1907)

I Hear America Singing

I hear America singing, the varied carols I hear,
Those of the mechanics, each singing his as it should be
    blithe and strong,
The carpenter singing his as he measures his plank or beam,
The mason singing his as he makes ready for work or leaves
    off work,
The boatman singing what belongs to him in his boat, the
    deck hand singing on the steamboat deck,
The shoemaker singing as he sits on his bench, the hatter
    singing as he stands,
The wood-cutter's song, the ploughboy's on his way in the
    morning, or at noon intermission or at sundown,
The delicious singing of the mother, or the young wife at
    work, or the girl sewing or washing,
Each sings what belongs to him or her and to none else,
The day what belongs to the day—at night the party of
    young fellows, robust, friendly,
Singing with open mouths their strong melodious songs.
                                    —WALT WHITMAN (1819–1892)

A Supermarket in California

What thoughts I have of you tonight, Walt Whitman, for I walked down the sidestreets under the trees with a headache self-conscious looking at the full moon.

In my hungry fatigue, and shopping for images, I went into the neon fruit supermarket, dreaming of your enumerations!

What peaches and what penumbras! Whole families shopping at night! Aisles full of husbands! Wives in the avocados, babies in the tomatoes! — and you, Garcia Lorca, what were you doing down by the watermelons?

I saw you, Walt Whitman, childless, lonely old grubber, poking among the meats in the refrigerator and eyeing the grocery boys.

I heard you asking questions of each: Who killed the pork chops? What price bananas? Are you my Angel?

I wandered in and out of the brilliant stacks of cans following you, and followed in my imagination by the store detective.

We strode down the open corridors together in our solitary fancy tasting artichokes, possessing every frozen delicacy, and never passing the cashier.

Where are we going, Walt Whitman? The doors close in an hour. Which way does your beard point tonight?

(I touch your book and dream of our odyssey in the supermarket and feel absurd.)

Will we walk all night through solitary streets? The trees add shade to shade, lights out in the houses, we'll both be lonely.

Will we stroll dreaming of the lost America of love past blue automobiles in driveways, home to our silent cottage?

Ah, dear father, graybeard, lonely old courage-teacher, what America did you have when Charon quit poling his ferry and you got out on a smoking bank and stood watching the boat disappear on the black waters of Lethe?

—ALLEN GINSBERG (b. 1926)

The Preponderance

To me there appears an immense preponderance of virtue and happiness even in this world, wicked and miserable as it is represented.

JOHN ADAMS

Headless fountains
running loose,
I've killed some chickens
I've seen a goose
I've thought of people
cut up for soap
but there's more to this
than chicken hope
or the chicken scare
that sells what's dear.

I read, I love
I eat, I drink
I watch the world tilt
I watch the children think:
there's so much to it
and most of it good
that while I've tendons
to lift my head,
like a rooster drinking
I'll nod to God
and save despair
for when I'm dead.

—WILLIAM MEREDITH (b. 1919)

In Goya's Greatest Scenes

In Goya's greatest scenes we seem to see
                              the people of the world
        exactly at the moment when
              they first attained the title of
                              "suffering humanity"
          They writhe upon the page
                        in a veritable rage
                                  of adversity

Heaped up
                    groaning with babies and bayonets
                        under cement skies
        in an abstract landscape of blasted trees
            bent statues bats wings and beaks
                    slippery gibbets
            cadavers and carnivorous cocks
        and all the final hollering monsters
            of the
                    "imagination of disaster"
            they are so bloody real
                    it is as if they really still existed

    And they do

            Only the landscape is changed

    They still are ranged along the roads
        plagued by legionnaires
                    false windmills and demented roosters

    They are the same people
                        only further from home
        on freeways fifty lanes wide
                    on a concrete continent
                        spaced with bland billboards
                illustrating imbecile illusions of happiness

    The scene shows fewer tumbrils
                        but more maimed citizens
                                in painted cars
            and they have strange license plates
        and engines
            that devour America
                    —LAWRENCE FERLINGHETTI (b. 1919)

The Latest Decalogue

        Thou shalt have one God only; who
        Would be at the expense of two?
        No graven images may be
        Worshipped, except the currency:

Swear not at all; for, for thy curse
Thine enemy is none the worse:
At church on Sunday to attend
Will serve to keep the world thy friend:
Honour thy parents; that is, all
From whom advancement may befall:
Thou shalt not kill; but need'st not strive
Officiously to keep alive:
Do not adultery commit;
Advantage rarely comes of it:
Thou shalt not steal; an empty feat,
When it's so lucrative to cheat:
Bear not false witness; let the lie
Have time on its own wings to fly:
Thou shalt not covet, but tradition
Approves all forms of competition.
            —ARTHUR HUGH CLOUGH (1819–1861)

The Inner Part

When they had won the war
And for the first time in history
Americans were the most important people—

When the leading citizens no longer lived in their shirt
        sleeves
And their wives did not scratch in public;
Just when they'd stopped saying "Gosh!"—

When their daughters seemed as sensitive
As the tip of a fly rod,
And their sons were as smooth as a V-8 engine—

Priests, examining the entrails of birds,
Found the heart misplaced, and seeds
As black as death, emitting a strange odor.
            —LOUIS SIMPSON (b. 1923)

Lines Written in Early Spring

I heard a thousand blended notes,
While in a grove I sate reclined,
In that sweet mood when pleasant thoughts
Bring sad thoughts to the mind.

To her fair works did Nature link
The human soul that through me ran;
And much it grieved my heart to think
What man has made of man.

Through primrose tufts, in that green bower,
The periwinkle trailed its wreaths;
And 'tis my faith that every flower
Enjoys the air it breathes.

The birds around me hopped and played,
Their thoughts I cannot measure:—
But the least motion which they made,
It seemed a thrill of pleasure.

The budding twigs spread out their fan,
To catch the breezy air;
And I must think, do all I can,
That there was pleasure there.

If this belief from heaven be sent,
If such be Nature's holy plan,
Have I not reason to lament
What man has made of man?
                    —WILLIAM WORDSWORTH (1770–1850)

Poem of Solitude at Columbia University

Back from a Walk

Heaven-murdered one,
among shapes turning serpent
and shapes seeking crystal,
I'll let my hair grow long.

With the tree-stump now tuneless
and the egg-white face of a child

With all crack-brained creatures
and the tatter of dry-footed water

With the deafmutes of torpor,
and the butterfly drowned in the inkwell

Shambling each day with my different face
Ah, heaven-murdered one!
—FEDERICO GARCIA LORCA (1898–1936)
TRANSLATED BY BEN BELITT (b. 1911)

Brooding

The sadness of our lives.
We will never be good enough to each other,
to our parents and friends.
We go along like old sailing ships,
loaded with food and drink for a long voyage,
self-sufficient, without any outside contact
with the world.
        The truth faces me
all the time. We are in a world
in which nobody listens to anybody,
in which we do as we please
until we are stopped by others.
We live our whole lives as in a husk,
which keeps us separate from any influence.
While those who reflect the influence
of others are either idiots, or people
who never gained consciousness.
—DAVID IGNATOW (b. 1914)

Meditatio

When I carefully consider the curious habits of dogs
I am compelled to conclude
That man is the superior animal.

When I consider the curious habits of man
I confess, my friend, I am puzzled.
—EZRA POUND (b. 1885)

Dolor

I have known the inexorable sadness of pencils,
Neat in their boxes, dolor of pad and paper-weight,
All the misery of manilla folders and mucilage,
Desolation in immaculate public places,
Lonely reception room, lavatory, switchboard,
The unalterable pathos of basin and pitcher,
Ritual of multigraph, paper-clip, comma,
Endless duplication of lives and objects.
And I have seen dust from the walls of institutions,
Finer than flour, alive, more dangerous than silica,
Sift, almost invisible, through long afternoons of tedium,
Dropping a fine film on nails and delicate eyebrows
Glazing the pale hair, the duplicate grey standard faces.
—THEODORE ROETHKE (1908–1963)

Meaning of Life

"*Hop and skip to fancy's fiddle,*
Hands across and down the middle,
Life's perhaps the only riddle
That we shrink from giving up."
—W. S. GILBERT

The Secret

Two girls discover
the secret of life
in a sudden line of
poetry.

I who don't know the
secret wrote
the line. They
told me

(Through a third person)
they had found it
but not what it was
not even

what line it was. No doubt
by now, more than a week
later, they have forgotten
the secret,

the line, the name of
the poem. I love them
for finding what
I can't find,

and for loving me
for the line I wrote,
and for forgetting it
so that

a thousand times, till death
finds them, they may
discover it again, in other
lines

in other
happenings. And for
wanting to know it,
for

assuming there is
such a secret, yes,
for that
most of all.

   —DENISE LEVERTOV (b. 1923)

The Fly

Little Fly,
Thy summer's play
My thoughtless hand
Has brush'd away.

Am not I
A fly like thee?
Or art not thou
A man like me?

For I dance,
And drink, & sing,
Till some blind hand
Shall brush my wing.

If thought is life
And strength & breath,
And the want
Of thought is death;

Then am I
A happy fly,
If I live
Or if I die.

   —WILLIAM BLAKE (1757–1827)

Responding Voice

Our life is not life, save in the fleeting
moments wrested from the barren task
of the daily struggle's paltry fray
that in its sameness likens men to brutes.

Our life is not life, save in the intense
instant that whips the flesh like a lightning flash,
that floods the spirit with the light of stars
and burns and strews it like a grain of incense.
>   —FRANCISCO A. DE ICAZA (1863–1925)
>   TRANSLATED BY SAMUEL BECKETT (b. 1906)

The Carpenter's Son

"Here the hangman stops his cart:
Now the best of friends must part.
Fare you well, for ill fare I:
Live, lads, and I will die.

"Oh, at home had I but stayed
'Prenticed to my father's trade,
Had I stuck to plane and adze,
I had not been lost, my lads.

"Then I might have built perhaps
Gallows-trees for other chaps,
Never dangled on my own,
Had I but left ill alone.

"Now, you see, they hang me high,
And the people passing by
Stop to shake their fists and curse;
So 'tis come from ill to worse.

"Here hang I, and right and left
Two poor fellows hang for theft:
All the same's the luck we prove,
Though the midmost hangs for love.

"Comrades all, that stand and gaze,
Walk henceforth in other ways;
See my neck and save your own:
Comrades all, leave ill alone.

"Make some day a decent end,
Shrewder fellows than your friend.
Fare you well, for ill fare I:
Live, lads, and I will die."
    —A. E. HOUSMAN (1859–1936)

I Saw a Man

I saw a man pursuing the horizon;
Round and round they sped.
I was disturbed at this;
I accosted the man.
"It is futile," I said,
"You can never"—

"You lie," he cried,
And ran on.
    —STEPHEN CRANE (1871–1900)

Vanity of Vanities

Vanity of vanities, saith the Preacher, vanity of vanities; all
    is vanity.
What profit hath a man of all his labour which he taketh
    under the sun?
One generation passeth away, and *another* generation cometh:
    but the earth abideth forever.
The sun also ariseth, and the sun goeth down, and hasteth
    to his place where he arose.
The wind goeth toward the south, and turneth about unto the
    north; it whirleth about continually, and the wind re-
    turneth again according to his circuits.
All the rivers run into the sea; yet the sea *is* not full; unto
    the place from whence the rivers come, thither they
    return again.
All things *are* full of labour; man cannot utter *it*: the eye is
    not satisfied with seeing, nor the ear filled with hearing.
The thing that hath been, it is *that* which shall be; and that
    which is done *is* that which shall be done: and *there is*
    no new *thing* under the sun.

Is there *any* thing of which it may be said, See this *is* new?
    it hath been already of old time, which was before us.
There is no remembrance of former *things*; neither shall
    there be *any* remembrance of *things* that are to come
    with *those* that shall come after.

ECCLESIASTES 1:2–11

Hap

If but some vengeful god would call to me
From up the sky, and laugh: "Thou suffering thing,
Know that thy sorrow is my ecstasy,
That thy love's loss is my hate's profiting!"

Then would I bear it, clench myself, and die,
Steeled by the sense of ire unmerited;
Half-eased in that a Powerfuller than I
Had willed and meted me the tears I shed.

But not so. How arrives it joy lies slain,
And why unblooms the best hope ever sown?
    Crass Casualty obstructs the sun and rain,
And dicing Time for gladness casts a moan . . .
These purblind Doomsters had as readily strown
Blisses about my pilgrimage as pain.

—THOMAS HARDY (1840–1928)

Musée des Beaux Arts

About suffering they were never wrong,
The Old Masters: how well they understood
Its human position; how it takes place
While someone else is eating or opening a window or just
    walking dully along;
How, when the aged are reverently, passionately waiting
For the miraculous birth, there always must be
Children who did not specially want it to happen, skating
On a pond at the edge of the wood:
They never forgot
That even the dreadful martyrdom must run its course
Anyhow in a corner, some untidy spot

Where the dogs go on with their doggy life and the torturer's
    horse
Scratches its innocent behind on a tree.
In Brueghel's *Icarus,* for instance: how everything turns away
Quite leisurely from the disaster; the ploughman may
Have heard the splash, the forsaken cry,
But for him it was not an important failure; the sun shone
As it had to on the white legs disappearing into the green
Water; and the expensive delicate ship that must have seen
Something amazing, a boy falling out of the sky,
Had somewhere to get to and sailed calmly on.

                  —W. H. AUDEN (b. 1907)

When I Have Fears That I May Cease to Be

When I have fears that I may cease to be
   Before my pen has gleaned my teeming brain,
Before high-pilèd books, in charact'ry,
   Hold like rich garners the full-ripened grain;
When I behold, upon the night's starred face,
   Huge cloudy symbols of a high romance,
And think that I may never live to trace

   Their shadows, with the magic hand of chance;
And when I feel, fair creature of an hour!
   That I shall never look upon thee more,
Never have relish in the faery power
   Of unreflecting love!—then on the shore
Of the wide world I stand alone, and think
Till love and fame to nothingness do sink.

                  —JOHN KEATS (1795–1821)

There Was a Child Went Forth

There was a child went forth every day,
And the first object he look'd upon, that object he became,
And that object became part of him for the day or a certain
    part of the day,
Or for many years or stretching cycles of years.

The early lilacs became part of this child,

And grass and white and red morning-glories, and white and red clover, and the song of the phœbe-bird,

And the Third-month lambs and the sow's pink-faint litter, and the mare's foal and the cow's calf,

And the noisy brood of the barnyard or by the mire of the pond-side,

And the fish suspending themselves so curiously below there, and the beautiful curious liquid,

And the water-plants with their graceful flat heads, all became part of him.

The field-sprouts of Fourth-month and Fifth-month became part of him,

Winter-grain sprouts and those of the light-yellow corn, and the esculent roots of the garden,

And the apple-trees cover'd with blossoms and the fruit afterward, and wood-berries, and the commonest weeds by the road,

And the old drunkard staggering home from the outhouse of the tavern whence he had lately risen,

And the schoolmistress that pass'd on her way to the school,

And the friendly boys that pass'd, and the quarrelsome boys,

And the tidy and fresh-cheek'd girls, and the barefoot Negro boy and girl,

And all the changes of city and country wherever he went.

His own parents, he that had father'd him and she that had conceiv'd him in her womb and birth'd him,

They gave this child more of themselves than that,

They gave him afterward every day, they became part of him.

The mother at home quietly placing the dishes on the supper-table,

The mother with mild words, clean her cap and gown, a wholesome odor falling off her person and clothes as she walks by,

The father, strong, self-sufficient, manly, mean, anger'd, unjust,

The blow, the quick loud word, the tight bargain, the crafty lure,

The family usages, the language, the company, the furniture, the yearning and swelling heart,

Affection that will not be gainsay'd, the sense of what is real, the thought if after all it should prove unreal,

The doubts of day-time and the doubts of night-time, the
    curious whether and how,
Whether that which appears so is so, or is it all flashes and
    specks?
Men and women crowding fast in the streets, if they are not
    flashes and specks what are they?
The streets themselves and the façades of houses, and goods
    in the windows,
Vehicles, teams, the heavy-plank'd wharves, the huge crossing
    at the ferries,
The village of the highland seen from afar at sunset, the river
    between,
Shadows, aureola and mist, the light falling on roofs and
    gables of white or brown two miles off,
The schooner near by sleepily dropping down the tide, the
    little boat slack-tow'd astern,
The hurrying tumbling waves, quick-broken crests, slapping,
The strata of color'd clouds, the long bar of maroon-tint
    away solitary by itself, the spread of purity it lies mo-
    tionless in,
The horizon's edge, the flying sea-crow, the fragrance of salt
    marsh and shore mud,
These became part of that child who went forth every day,
    and who now goes, and will always go forth every day.
            —WALT WHITMAN (1819–1892)

On His Seventy-Fifth Birthday

I strove with none, for none was worth my strife.
    Nature I loved and, next to Nature, Art:
I warmed both hands before the fire of life;
    It sinks, and I am ready to depart.
           —WALTER SAVAGE LANDOR (1775–1864)

Ode
Intimations of Immortality from Recollections of Early Childhood

I

There was a time when meadow, grove, and stream,
The earth, and every common sight,

To me did seem
　　Apparelled in celestial light,
The glory and the freshness of a dream.
It is not now as it hath been of yore;—
　　　Turn wheresoe'er I may,
　　　　By night or day,
The things which I have seen I now can see no more.

II

　　　The Rainbow comes and goes,
　　　　And lovely is the Rose;
　　　The Moon doth with delight
Look round her when the heavens are bare;
　　　Waters on a starry night
　　　Are beautiful and fair;
　The sunshine is a glorious birth;
　But yet I know, where'er I go,
That there hath past away a glory from the earth.

III

Now, while the birds thus sing a joyous song,
　　And while the young lambs bound
　　　As to the tabor's sound,
To me alone there came a thought of grief;
A timely utterance gave that thought relief,
　　And I again am strong:
The cataracts blow their trumpets from the steep;
No more shall grief of mine the season wrong;
I hear the Echoes through the mountains throng,
The Winds come to me from the fields of sleep,
　　　And all the earth is gay;
　　　　Land and sea
　Give themselves up to jollity,
　　　And with the heart of May
Doth every Beast keep holiday;—
　　　Thou Child of Joy,
Shout round me, let me hear thy shouts, thou happy
　Shepherd-boy!

IV

Ye blessèd Creatures, I have heard the call
　　Ye to each other make; I see
The heavens laugh with you in your jubilee;
　　My heart is at your festival,

My head hath its coronal,
The fullness of your bliss, I feel—I feel it all.
　Oh evil day! if I were sullen
　While Earth herself is adorning,
　　This sweet May-morning,
　And the Children are culling
　　On every side,
　In a thousand valleys far and wide,
　Fresh flowers; while the sun shines warm,
And the Babe leaps up on his Mother's arm:—
　I hear, I hear, with joy I hear!
　—But there's a Tree, of many, one,
A single Field which I have looked upon,
Both of them speak of something that is gone:
　The Pansy at my feet
　Doth the same tale repeat:
Whither is fled the visionary gleam?
Where is it now, the glory and the dream?

V

Our birth is but a sleep and a forgetting:
The Soul that rises with us, our life's Star,
　Hath had elsewhere its setting,
　　And cometh from afar:
　Not in entire forgetfulness,
　And not in utter nakedness,
But trailing clouds of glory do we come
　From God, who is our home;
Heaven lies about us in our infancy!
Shades of the prison-house begin to close
　　Upon the growing Boy,
But He beholds the light, and whence it flows,
　　He sees it in his joy;
　The Youth, who daily farther from the east
　　Must travel, still is Nature's Priest,
　　And by the vision splendid
　　Is on his way attended;
　At length the Man perceives it die away,
　And fade into the light of common day.

VI

Earth fills her lap with pleasures of her own;
Yearnings she hath in her own natural kind,
And, even with something of a Mother's mind,

And no unworthy aim,
    The homely Nurse doth all she can
To make her Foster-child, her Inmate Man,
    Forget the glories he hath known,
And that imperial palace whence he came.

VII

Behold the Child among his new-born blisses,
A six years' Darling of a pigmy size!
See, where 'mid work of his own hand he lies,
Fretted by sallies of his mother's kisses,
With light upon him from his father's eyes!
See, at his feet, some little plan or chart,
Some fragment from his dream of human life,
Shaped by himself with newly-learnèd art;
        A wedding or a festival,
        A mourning or a funeral;
            And this hath now his heart,
            And unto this he frames his song;
        Then will he fit his tongue
To dialogues of business, love, or strife;
        But it will not be long
        Ere this be thrown aside,
        And with new joy and pride
The little Actor cons another part;
Filling from time to time his "humorous stage"
With all the Persons, down to palsied Age,
That Life brings with her in her equipage;
    As if his whole vocation
    Were endless imitation.

VIII

Thou, whose exterior semblance doth belie
    Thy Soul's immensity;
Thou best Philosopher, who yet dost keep
Thy heritage, thou Eye among the blind,
That, deaf and silent, read'st the eternal deep,
Haunted for ever by the eternal mind,—
    Mighty Prophet! Seer blest!
    On whom those truths do rest,
Which we are toiling all our lives to find,
In darkness lost, the darkness of the grave;
Thou, over whom thy Immortality
Broods like the Day, a Master o'er a Slave,

A Presence which is not to be put by;
Thou little Child, yet glorious in the might
Of heaven-born freedom on thy being's height,
Why with such earnest pains dost thou provoke
The years to bring the inevitable yoke,
Thus blindly with thy blessedness at strife?
Full soon thy Soul shall have her earthly freight,
And custom lie upon thee with a weight,
Heavy as frost, and deep almost as life!

IX

    O joy! that in our embers
    Is something that doth live,
    That nature yet remembers
    What was so fugitive!
The thought of our past years in me doth breed
Perpetual benediction: not indeed
For that which is most worthy to be blessed—
Delight and liberty, the simple creed
Of Childhood, whether busy or at rest,
With new-fledged hope still fluttering in his breast:—
      Not for these I raise
      The song of thanks and praise;
    But for those obstinate questionings
    Of sense and outward things,
    Fallings from us, vanishings;
    Blank misgivings of a Creature
Moving about in worlds not realized,
High instincts before which our mortal Nature
Did tremble like a guilty Thing surprised:
      But for those first affections,
      Those shadowy recollections,
    Which, be they what they may,
Are yet the fountain light of all our day,
Are yet a master light of all our seeing;
    Uphold us, cherish, and have power to make
Our noisy years seem moments in the being
Of the eternal Silence: truths that wake,
      To perish never;
Which neither listlessness, nor mad endeavor,
      Nor Man nor Boy,
Nor all that is at enmity with joy,
Can utterly abolish or destroy!
      Hence in a season of calm weather

Though inland far we be,
Our Souls have sight of that immortal sea
  Which brought us hither,
  Can in a moment travel thither,
And see the Children sport upon the shore,
And hear the mighty waters rolling evermore.

    X

Then sing, ye Birds, sing, sing a joyous song!
  And let the young Lambs bound
  As to the tabor's sound!
We in thought will join your throng,
  Ye that pipe and ye that play,
  Ye that through your hearts to-day
  Feel the gladness of the May!
What though the radiance which was once so bright
Be now for ever taken from my sight,
  Though nothing can bring back the hour
Of splendour in the grass, of glory in the flower;
  We will grieve not, rather find
  Strength in what remains behind;
  In the primal sympathy
  Which having been must ever be;
  In the soothing thoughts that spring
  Out of human suffering;
  In the faith that looks through death,
In years that bring the philosophic mind.

    XI

And O, ye Fountains, Meadows, Hills, and Groves,
Forebode not any severing of our loves!
Yet in my heart of hearts I feel your might;
I only have relinquished one delight
To live beneath your more habitual sway.
I love the Brooks which down their channels fret,
Even more than when I tripped lightly as they;
The innocent brightness of a new-born Day
  Is lovely yet;
The Clouds that gather round the setting sun
Do take a sober colouring from an eye
That hath kept watch o'er man's mortality;
Another race hath been, and other palms are won.
Thanks to the human heart by which we live,
Thanks to its tenderness, its joys, and fears,

To me the meanest flower that blows can give
Thoughts that do often lie too deep for tears.
                    —WILLIAM WORDSWORTH (1770–1850)

If I Should Cast Off This Tattered Coat

If I should cast off this tattered coat,
And go free into the mighty sky;
If I should find nothing there
But a vast blue,
Echoless, ignorant—
What then?
                    —STEPHEN CRANE (1871–1900)

Dover Beach

The sea is calm tonight,
The tide is full, the moon lies fair
Upon the straits;—on the French coast the light
Gleams and is gone; the cliffs of England stand,
Glimmering and vast, out in the tranquil bay.
Come to the window, sweet is the night-air!
Only, from the long line of spray
Where the sea meets the moon-blanched land,
Listen! you hear the grating roar
Of pebbles which the waves draw back, and fling,
At their return, up the high strand,
Begin, and cease, and then again begin,
With tremulous cadence slow, and bring
The eternal note of sadness in.

Sophocles long ago
Heard it on the Aegean, and it brought
Into his mind the turbid ebb and flow
Of human misery; we
Find also in the sound a thought,
Hearing it by this distant northern sea.

The Sea of Faith
Was once, too, at the full, and round earth's shore

turbid, clouded.

Lay like the folds of a bright girdle furled.
But now I only hear
Its melancholy, long, withdrawing roar,
Retreating, to the breath
Of the night-wind, down the vast edges drear
And naked shingles of the world.

Ah, love, let us be true
To one another! for the world, which seems
To lie before us like a land of dreams,
So various, so beautiful, so new,
Hath really neither joy, nor love, nor light,
Nor certitude, nor peace, nor help for pain;
And we are here as on a darkling plain
Swept with confused alarms of struggle and flight,
Where ignorant armies clash by night.

—MATTHEW ARNOLD (1822–1888)

A Life

Innocence?
In a sense.
In no sense!

Was that *it?*
Was *that* it?
Was that it?

That was it.

—HOWARD NEMEROV (b. 1920)

shingles, pebbled shores.

Prosody

A GLOSSARY OF POETIC TERMS

Prosody

A Glossary of Poetic Terms

Examples given are from poems that can be found in this volume.

ALLEGORY: A work in which a literal meaning parallels or symbolizes a deeper meaning, often moral or didactic. See, for example, Samuel Taylor Coleridge, "Time, Real and Imaginary," page 194.

ALLITERATION: The repetition of consonant sounds within a line or stanza, especially initial consonants.

> "We passed the fields of *gazing grain,*
> We passed the *setting sun.*"
> —from Emily Dickinson, "Because I Could Not Stop for Death"

AMPHIBRACH (adjective, AMPHIBRACHIC): A metrical foot of three syllables, unaccented, accented, unaccented.

> "Wăs thát ĭt?"
> —from Nemerov, "A Life"

ANAPEST (adjective, ANAPESTIC): A metrical foot of three syllables, two unaccented syllables followed by an accented one, giving an effect of rapid rhythm. The following is anapestic tetrameter.

> "Lĭke thĕ leaves/ŏf thĕ for/ĕst whĕn Sūm/mĕr ĭs green. . . ."
> —from Byron, "The Destruction of Sennacherib"

ANTITHESIS: A figure of speech balancing one thought with a contrasting thought, such as "Man proposes, but God disposes," or:

> "The best lack all conviction, while the worst
> Are full of passionate intensity."
> —from Yeats, "The Second Coming"

APOSTROPHE: A figure of speech addressing someone absent as if present or an object, an abstract quality, or a non-existent being, as if it were a living thing.

"Milton! Thou shouldst be living at this hour. . . ."
—from Wordsworth, "London, 1802"

ASSONANCE: Semirhyme in which vowel sounds are matched but the consonants following them are not. For example, *moot* and *loot* are true rhymes; *sneak* and *steal* are assonant. See *Rhyme*.

BALLAD: A narrative in which a popular romantic, amusing, tender, or tragic story is told. Among the common features are swift action, little or no explanation of character or events, simplicity of structure, frequent use of dialogue, ballad stanza form, refrains, superstition. "The Riddling Knight" on page 81 is an example of a popular ballad whose author is unknown and whose source is probably communal. The literary or art ballad is the work of a single poet adopting the characteristics of the popular ballad. See, for example, Edna St. Vincent Millay, "The Ballad of the Harp Weaver," page 102.

BALLAD STANZA: The ballad stanza consists of four lines, usually of alternating iambic tetrameter and iambic trimeter, with the rhyme scheme *abab* or *abcb*.

The first/word that/Sir Pa/trick read,
A loud/laugh laugh/ed he;
The next/word that/Sir Pa/trick read,
The tear/blinded/his e'e.

—from "Sir Patrick Spens"

COUPLET: Two consecutive rhymed lines.

"Had we but world enough, and time,
This coyness, Lady, were no crime."

—from Marvell, "To His Coy Mistress"

DACTYL (adjective, DACTYLIC): A metrical foot consisting of one accented syllable, followed by two unaccented syllables, usually with a lilting effect as in the word "merrily" which is itself a dactylic foot.

"Not with a/bang but a/whimper."

—from Eliot, "The Hollow Men"

DIMETER: A metrical line of two feet. For example:

> "I'll nŏd/tŏ Gŏd
> ănd săve/dĕspair
> fŏr whĕn/I'm dĕad."
>
> —from William Meredith, "The Preponderance"

DRAMATIC MONOLOGUE: A lyric poem in which one character has a dramatic, one-way conversation with another. See, for example, Robert Browning, "My Last Duchess," page 71.

ELEGY: A poem of mourning for the dead. See, for example, Thomas Gray, "Elegy Written in a Country Churchyard," page 235, though the grief expressed in this famous elegy is more broadly for life's disappointments.

END RHYME: Rhyme which occurs at the end of lines, as opposed to internal rhyme.

> "The wind flapped loose, the wind was still,
> Shaken out dead from tree and hill. . . ."
>
> —from Rossetti, "The Woodspurge"

EPIGRAM: A short poem expressing an idea in polished (often witty) and succinct terms. See, for example, Pound, "Meditatio," page 271.

FEMININE ENDING: An extra syllable, unstressed, added to the end of a metrical line in iambic or anapestic meter. It's an irregularity that adds lightness to a line. For example:

> "Whĕn I/wăs ŏne/-ănd-twĕn/tў
> I hĕard/ă wise/măn say . . ."
>
> —from Housman, "When I Was One-and-Twenty"

FIGURE OF SPEECH: A word, phrase, or even an entire poem used imaginatively rather than literally to create a more vivid or stronger effect. See: *Allegory, Antithesis, Apostrophe, Hyperbole, Irony, Litotes, Metaphor, Metonymy, Oxymoron, Paradox, Simile, Synecdoche.*

FOOT: A measure of rhythm, an accent pattern. A metrical unit of one, two, or three syllables usually with one of these being stressed, the other(s) unstressed. See: *Amphibrach, Anapest, Dactyl, Iamb, Spondee, Trochee.*

FREE VERSE: Verse without a regular metrical or rhyming pattern; see, for example, Walt Whitman, "A Noiseless Patient Spider," page 248.

HEPTAMETER: A metrical line of seven feet.
" 'What are/the bu/gles blow/in' for?'/says Fi/les on/Parade.
'To turn/you out,/to turn/you out,/' the Col/or Sar/geant said."
　　　　　　　　　　　　—from Kipling, "Danny Deever"

HAIKU: A lyric poem of seventeen syllables divided into three lines. From Japanese poetry. See, for example, José Tablada, "Haiku," page 42.

HEXAMETER: A metrical line of six feet.
"And con/summa/tion comes,/and jars/two hem/ispheres."
　　　　　　　—from Hardy, "The Convergence of the Twain"

HYPERBOLE: A figure of speech using strong and intentional exaggeration.
For example:
　　　　　"I'll love you, dear, I'll love you
　　　　　　　Till China and Africa meet,
　　　　And the river jumps over the mountain
　　　　　　And the salmon sing in the street"
　　　　　—from Auden, "As I Walked Out One Evening"

IAMB (adjective, IAMBIC): The most common metrical foot in English verse, consisting of an unaccented syllable followed by an accented one.
"My eyes/grew dim,/and I/could no/more gaze. . . ."
　　　　　　　—from McKay, "The Tropics in New York"

INTERNAL RHYME: Rhyme occurring within a line:
"For your brain is on *fire*—the bedclothes con*spire* of usual *slumber* to *plunder* you. . . ."
　　　　　　　　　　　—from Gilbert, "Nightmare"

IRONY: A figure of speech in which the real meaning of a statement is the opposite of its literal meaning, as when praise is expressed but criticism implied. In a deeper sense, irony implies an awareness of the gaps between how things are and how things seem (or should be). For example, in David Ignatow's "Two Friends" (page 132), the title is ironic in relation to the poem.

LIGHT VERSE: A broad term covering poetry which ranges from nonsense to highly polished, witty verse, such as Phyllis McGinley's "The Giveaway" on page 63.

LITOTES: A figure of speech in which an affirmative is expressed by the negation of its opposite ("You are not a bad shot."). Sometimes the term means understatement (the opposite of hyperbole) as in poetry:

> "Yes; quaint and curious war is!"
>
> —from Hardy, "The Man He Killled"

LYRIC: A short subjective poem, marked by emotion and unity of effect and often of a highly personal nature. For example, "Cuckoo Song" on page 32 or D. H. Lawrence's "A Young Wife" on page 129.

METAPHOR: A figure of speech in which two things usually not associated together are compared implicitly, without using the "like" or "as" that characterizes similes. "The sun is like a brave man" would be a simile. The following is metaphor, a stronger form of comparison:

> "The sun, that brave man,
> Comes through boughs that lie in wait. . . ."
>
> —from Stevens, "The Brave Man"

METER: The measure of a rhythm established by the regular (or almost regular) recurrence of a definite pattern of stressed and unstressed syllables (each patterned set of syllables referred to as a metrical foot). The most common metrical feet (see elsewhere in glossary) are Iambs ($\smile$ —), Trochees (— $\smile$), Dactyls (— $\smile$ $\smile$), Anapests ($\smile$ $\smile$ —), Amphibrachs ($\smile$ — $\smile$), and Spondees (— —). One defines the meter of the poem—the mechanical means by which a poet achieves his effects—by describing both the type of accent pattern used (the foot) and the number of feet in a line. A verse of one foot (of any kind) is called *monometer;* of two feet, *dimeter;* of three, *trimeter;* four, *tetrameter;* five, *pentameter;* six, *hexameter;* seven, *heptameter;* eight, *octameter.* A verse in which the lines consist of five iambic feet, for example, is called *iambic pentameter,* as in:

"My eyes/grew dim,/and I/could no/more gaze. . . ."

—from McKay, "The Tropics in New York"

METONYMY: A form of comparison which substitutes one word for another with which it is closely associated. In the following, "sceptre" and "crown" represent royalty; "in the dust," death; "scythe" and "spade," the laboring peasant.

> "*Sceptre* and *Crown*
> Must tumble down,
> And *in the dust* be equal made
> With the *poor crooked scythe and spade.*"

—from Shirley, "Death the Leveller"

MONOMETER: A line of verse of one metrical foot.

"And swear
No where. . . ."

—from Donne, "Song"

NARRATIVE POETRY: Poetry that stresses plot, incident, and action. For example, "The Golden Vanity" on page 96.

OCTAVE or OCTET: Eight lines of a poem—especially the first eight lines of an Italian or Petrarchan sonnet. See *Sonnet.* For example, William Wordsworth, "The World Is Too Much with Us," page 250.

ODE: An elaborate lyric poem in exalted style, often addressed to a praised person, thing, or quality. For example, William Wordsworth, "Ode on Intimations of Immortality," page 282.

ONOMATOPOEIA: A word or the use of a word whose sound suggests its meaning (e.g., "buzz," "murmuring").

"The plopping of the waterdrops. . . ."

—from Amy Lowell, "Patterns"

OXYMORON: A rhetorical device in which two apparently contradictory words are brought together to express a truth, or for dramatic effect, as with "armless ambidextrian."

—from MacLeish, "End of the World"

PARADOX: A statement which, apparently contradictory, may actually be true:

> "For thus,—a paradox
> Which comforts while it mocks,—
> . . . What I aspired to be,
> And was not, comforts me. . . ."

> > —from Browning, "Rabbi Ben Ezra"

PARODY: A work that mimics an author's style or thought, usually by the humorous treatment of a trivial theme. See Ogden Nash, "Love under the Republicans (Or Democrats)," page 109.

PENTAMETER: A metric line of five feet (in this case, iambic pentameter):

> "A speck/that would/have been/beneath/my sight. . . ."

> > —from Frost, "A Considerable Speck"

PERSONIFICATION: A figure of speech in which human qualities are attributed to animals, inanimate objects, or abstractions.

> "A narrow wind complains all day
> How someone treated him. . . ."

> > —from Emily Dickinson, "The Sky Is Low,
> > the Clouds Are Mean"

QUATRAIN: The most common stanza form, consisting of four lines. For example, see Matthew Arnold, "The Last Word," page 206.

QUINTAIN or QUINTET: A stanza of five lines. For example, Henry Wadsworth Longfellow, "The Tide Rises, the Tide Falls," page 30.

REFRAIN: A phrase, line, couplet, or quatrain which recurs at intervals throughout the poem: For example:

> "So long,
> So far away,
> Is Africa."

> > —from Hughes, "Afro-American Fragment"

RHYME: Similarity or identity of the accented and terminal syllables of two words. For example, in the next entry rhymes are italicized. See: *End Rhyme, Internal Rhyme, Assonance, Rhyme Scheme.*

RHYME SCHEME: The pattern in which rhymes are arranged in a poem, in this case *a a b c c c b*.

> "It seems vainglorious and *proud*   a
> Of Atom-man to boast *aloud*   a
>   His prowess *homicidal*   b
> When one remembers how for *years*   c
> With their rude stones and humble *spears*,   c
> Our sires, at wiping out their *peers*,   c
>   Were almost never idle."   b

—Phyllis McGinley, "The Conquerors"

RHYTHM: The sense of flow and movement that comes with a rise and fall in emphasis, in regular or irregular patterns. Loosely, the same as *beat*, though beat specifically refers to the heavy accent. *Meter* refers to the measuring of accents and feet in poetry. (See *Meter*.)

SATIRE: A form of writing that ridicules or criticizes with humor or wit, often with social reform in mind. For example, Arthur Hugh Clough, "The Latest Decalogue," page 269.

SESTET: A stanza constituting the last six lines of an Italian or Petrarchan sonnet. See *Sonnet*. For example, William Wordsworth, "The World Is Too Much with Us," page 250.

SIMILE: A figure of speech in which two essentially unlike things with one striking similarity are compared directly, using the words "like" or "as." (See also *Metaphor*.)

> "When their daughters seemed as sensitive
> As the tip of a fly rod,
> And their sons were as smooth as a V-8 engine. . . ."

—from Simpson, "The Inner Part"

SONNET: A poem of fourteen lines written in iambic pentameter and expressing a single idea or emotion. The Italian or Petrarchan sonnet is composed of an octave (eight lines) with the rhyme scheme *abbaabba*, followed by a sestet (six lines) in which the rhyme scheme may vary, often being *cdcdcd* or *cdecde*. The octave presents a situation, raises a question, or makes a proposition; the sestet resolves the tension created by the octave by generalizing about the situation, answering the question, applying the proposition, etc. For example: George Gordon Byron, "Sonnet on Chillon," page 210. The Elizabethan or Shakespearean sonnet is composed of three quatrains and a concluding couplet with the rhyme scheme *ababcdcdefefgg*. For example, Shakespeare, "Let Me Not to the Marriage of True Minds," page 116.

SPONDEE (adjective, SPONDAIC): A metrical foot composed of two equally accented syllables, used for emphasis or to suggest gravity.

> "Late, late,/yestreen. . . ."
> —from "Sir Patrick Spens"

STANZA: An arrangement of two, three, four, or more lines of verse in a fixed metrical and rhyming pattern. See: *Ballad Stanza, Couplet, Octave, Quatrain, Sestet, Terza Rima, Tercet or Triplet.*

SYMBOL: A material object or person used to represent an idea, an event, or a relationship.

> "I warmed both hands before the fire of life,
> It sinks, and I am ready to depart."
> —from Landor, "On His Seventy-Fifth Birthday"

SYNECDOCHE: A figure of speech in which a part is used for the whole or the whole for a part.

> "The hand that signed the paper
> felled a city. . . ."
> —from Thomas, "The Hand That Signed the Paper"

TERZA RIMA: A group of three-line stanzas with interlinking rhymes: *aba bcb cdc*, etc. For example, Karl Shapiro, "Interlude," page 240.

TETRAMETER: A metrical line of four feet:

> "She walks/in beau/ty, like/the night. . . ."
> —from Byron, "She Walks in Beauty"

TRIMETER: A metrical line of three feet. In the following, the first line also has a feminine ending. (See *Feminine Ending.*)

> "When I/was one/-and-twen/ty
> I heard/a wise/man say. . . ."
> —from Housman, "When I Was One-and-Twenty"

TRIPLET or TERCET: A stanza of three lines usually rhyming *aaa*. See, for example, Thomas Hardy, "The Convergence of the Twain," page 98.

TROCHEE (adjective, TROCHAIC): A metrical foot consisting of one accented syllable followed by one unaccented. In a trochaic line the last syllable is often omitted.

"Glory/be to/God for/dappled/things. . . ."
—from Hopkins, "Pied Beauty"

About the Poets

ARNOLD, MATTHEW (1822–1888), English poet, educator, and critic, was the son of the famous headmaster at Rugby. He studied at Rugby and then Oxford, where he eventually became Professor of Poetry. All of his poetry was written in his early years. In his later years he concentrated on and elevated to a high level the art of literary and social criticism.

AUDEN, WYSTAN HUGH (1907–1973), born in York, England, became part of a literary circle that included Stephen Spender, Louis MacNeice, and Christopher Isherwood, writers and poets noted for their great concern over the critical social and political problems of the 1930s. Auden came to New York in 1939 and became a naturalized citizen by 1956. His early work is classed as the poetry of revolt, but he later converted from liberal-humanism to orthodox Anglicanism.

BECKETT, SAMUEL (b. 1906), novelist, poet, translator, and dramatist, was born in Dublin but has spent most of his life in Paris. The major part of his work has been written in French. He served for a time as secretary to James Joyce, sharing his preoccupation with language and with the failure of human beings to successfully communicate, thus mirroring the pointlessness of life which they strive to make purposeful. Beckett is best known for his play, *Waiting for Godot*. In 1969, he was awarded the Nobel Prize for Literature.

BELITT, BEN (b. 1911), author, educator and translator, was born in New York City. He is now on the faculty of Bennington College in Vermont. Belitt has received numerous awards for poetry, including a Guggenheim Fellowship in 1946 and the National Institute of Arts and Letters Award in 1965.

BLAKE, WILLIAM (1757–1827), the son of a London hosier, was apprenticed at the age of fourteen to an engraver. Later, he illustrated and engraved his own works as well as those of other poets. All through his life he upheld the belief in visitations from the outside world. His ardent belief in the freedom of the imagination and his hatred of rationalism and materialism have gained him the title of visionary poet. Even now, much time is devoted to the study of his mystical symbolism.

BRINTON, DANIEL GARRISON (1837–1899), archeologist and linguist, was born in Chester, Pennsylvania, and was graduated from Yale University and Jefferson Medical College. He published translations and studies of Mayan poetry.

BROOKS, GWENDOLYN (b. 1917), was born in Topeka, Kansas, and grew up in the ghetto slums of Chicago. She contributed poems to the black newspaper the *Defender,* and was awarded a Pulitzer Prize in poetry and two Guggenheim Fellowships. She is the author of the novel *Maud Martha.*

BROWNING, ELIZABETH BARRETT (1806–1861), is best known for her two most successful poems, *Sonnets from the Portuguese* and *Aurora Leigh.* An early riding accident and weak lungs left her a semi-invalid, and after the fateful drowning of her favorite brother she went into a deep depression. She secretly fell in love with and married poet Robert Browning, both fleeing to Italy to live, as her father had expressly forbidden any of his daughters to marry. She died in Florence, having already received popular acclaim during her lifetime.

BROWNING, ROBERT (1812–1889), was an English poet whose masterpiece, *The Ring and the Book,* in which the poignant story was interpreted through dramatic monologues, displays an almost journalistic approach to poetry. His poetry is notable for its depth of spiritual insight and power of psychological analysis.

BURNS, ROBERT (1759–1796), was born in Ayrshire, Scotland, the son of a poor tenant farmer. His humble origin and his identification with the Scottish folk tradition, which he rescued and embellished, provide the reasons for his enduring popularity as the national poet of Scotland. It was as the satirical poet, the ironical observer of religion, politics, manners, and human nature, and the unromantic love poet of the folk tradition that he secured his place in literature.

BYRON, GEORGE GORDON, LORD (1788–1824), was one of the most celebrated men of his age for his poetry and his romantic and flamboyant temperament. Lame from birth, he was extraordinarily handsome and became notorious for his many love affairs and adventures. An English baron, he became involved in political activity, especially in the battle for Greek independence, and he died while aiding the Greek forces. His romantic and satirical poetry was very popular in his day, and he had a far-reaching influence both as the creator of the "Byronic hero" and as the champion of political liberty.

CARROLL, LEWIS (1832–1898), was the pen name for Charles Lutwidge Dodgson, a mathematics lecturer at Oxford for twenty-five years. He was a solitary deacon, a dull teacher, an amateur photographer, a clever logician, and an inspired teller of nonsense tales. He is best known for his books, *Alice's Adventures in Wonderland* and *Through the Looking-Glass*.

CARRYL, GUY WETMORE (1873–1904), American poet, was graduated from Columbia University in 1895. He did editorial work for various publishers, became a foreign correspondent and the Paris representative for the publishing firm of Harper and Brothers.

CHAUCER, GEOFFERY (c. 1340–1400), was one of the early giants of English literature. The son of a London vintner and tavern keeper, he held positions at court and traveled abroad under the patronage of John of Gaunt. He was influenced in his early work by French and Italian literature but his mature work, especially *The Canterbury Tales,* is of true English flavor.

CLARE, JOHN (1793–1864), the son of a poor English laborer, was a herdboy, unsuccessful farmer, and occasionally a vagrant. With practically no schooling he began writing verse, and his poems had a very good reception. He was confined until his death in an insane asylum at Northampton, and the poem in this collection, written during his confinement, parallels many modern expressions of alienation.

CLOUGH, ARTHUR HUGH (1819–1861), was the son of a Liverpool cotton merchant. He was educated at Oxford and later became an examiner in the education office. He was close friends with the great Victorians Ruskin, Arnold, and Carlyle, and with distinguished Americans in Boston, where he lived for a while. He was a precursor of "the Angry Young Men" of the post-World War II era in that he imbibed the revolutionary doctrine of George Sand, called himself a republican, and disliked class distinction and the capitalist system.

COLERIDGE, SAMUEL TAYLOR (1772–1834), was the son of an English vicar. With Robert Southey he tried to form a utopian society. Later he collaborated with Wordsworth on the historic volume, *Lyrical Ballads*. A landmark in English literature and the beginning of the nineteenth-century romantic movement, it upset the old literary standards and introduced a new type of character, the peasant, adapting the ballad form from folk songs of the countryside. Unfortunately, Coleridge acquired the opium habit and went through a dejected period where for many years he could write nothing and alienated his family and friends. He managed to recover to a large degree and in later years was considered not only a formidable poet but also a major literary critic.

COLLINS, WILLIAM (1721–1759), the son of a Chichester hatter, was unsuccessfully trying to earn a living by literature when he inherited a small fortune at age 28 and retired from London to his native town. While still in London, however, he wrote his *Odes*, one poem of which is said to have foreshadowed the whole romantic school. He died a complete unknown after long suffering with a mental disease.

CRANE, STEPHEN (1871–1900), a poet, novelist, and short story writer, was born in Newark, New Jersey, the last of fourteen children. His father was a Methodist minister, who sent him to Lafayette College and then to Syracuse University. A brilliant prodigy, he lived in New York City as a freelance writer with a keen eye for the details of life in the Bowery—with Crane, slums became literary material, thereby putting Naturalism onto the American scene. He traveled to Cuba and Greece as a war correspondent and died of tuberculosis at the age of 29. His most famous work was the novel *The Red Badge of Courage*.

CRUZ, VICTOR HERNANDEZ (b. 1949), was born in Puerto Rico and came to live in New York in 1952. He attended Benjamin Franklin High School where he began to write poetry. He is now working with the Gut Theatre in East Harlem.

CULLEN, COUNTEE (1903–1946), black American poet, attended De Witt Clinton High School in New York City and received his B.A. from New York University and his M.A. from Harvard. He received a Guggenheim Fellowship and lived for a while in Paris. With few exceptions, he limited himself to the English sonnet and traditional ballad forms. His contribution to the Harlem Renaissance was in the romantic attitude he took toward the African past.

CUMMINGS, EDWARD ESTLIN (1894–1962), American painter and writer, was born and raised in Massachusetts, the son of a well-known preacher and lecturer. He received his B.A. and M.A. from Harvard and then served in the ambulance corps in France during World War I. In presenting his poetic themes of nature, love, underdogs, and the blatant materialism of our time, he was a fearless experimenter, using every trick of typography to heighten his meaning.

DAVID, King of the Hebrews (c. 1012–972 B.C.), was the hero of many Biblical narratives. He slew the giant Goliath with his sling, was the friend of Jonathan and a favorite of King Saul, and is said to have written many Psalms. As their ruler, David united the Jewish tribes into a single kingdom.

DENSMORE, FRANCES (1867–1957), was born in Red Wing, Minnesota, and studied piano and harmony at Oberlin College. She has published many articles on Indian music and dance and has made translations of Indian poetry.

DICKINSON, EMILY (1830–1886), American poet born in Amherst, Massachusetts, was the daughter of a lawyer who became a congressman. She spent one year at South Hadley Female Seminary (now Mount Holyoke College) but left to lead a solitary existence, meeting rarely with a few intimate friends. Her lyrics are brief and usually concerned with the phenomena of nature, the themes of love, death, and immortality. After her death, over one thousand unpublished poems were discovered, which, with their originality of rhymes, metric forms, and varying poetic feet, have had a considerable influence on modern poetry.

DONNE, JOHN (1572–1631), the son of a London ironmonger, was converted from Catholicism to Anglicanism as a young man but was not ordained in the Church of England until his early forties. He became very famous in his day for sermons preached as Dean of St. Paul's Cathedral, but is best known today for his love poems and religious poetry. His influence on modern verse has been considerable, due mainly to the intellectual vigor of his work, his range of learned reference, and his wit, and he is regarded as an outstanding metaphysical poet.

DRAYTON, MICHAEL (1563–1631), born at Hartshill, Warwickshire, was a dedicated poet and collaborator on many plays. In his early and longest works, he aimed at celebrating England's glories. He later wrote pastoral poems and sonnets.

DRYDEN, JOHN (1631–1700), was born in Northamptonshire and educated at Cambridge. He wrote prolifically—verse, drama, satire, criticism, translations—and was made Poet Laureate and royal historiographer. Clarity and balance are keynotes of his style, and he is considered transitional between the metaphysical poets of the school of Donne and the neo-classic reaction which he did so much to create.

DUNBAR, PAUL LAURENCE (1872–1906), poet and novelist, was born in Dayton, Ohio, to former slaves. While working as an elevator boy in a Dayton hotel, he met and attracted the interest of William Dean Howells, one of the leading literary figures of the time. Dunbar achieved great popularity during his lifetime for his lyric poetry, which made use of dialect and folk material.

ELIOT, THOMAS STEARNS (1888–1965), was born in St. Louis and educated at Harvard, the Sorbonne, and Oxford. He became a British subject, converted to Catholicism, and in 1948 won the Nobel Prize for Literature. He wrote verse, drama, and criticism and has been one of the most influential poets of our time. His most famous poem, *The Wasteland,* became a symbol of the modern era, with its theme of the aridity of modern life and the horror of a civilization dying of spiritual drought. His criticisms, which appeared with equally important effect, were written from the Christian point of view, and his plays were often inspired by Catholic doctrine.

EVANS, MARI, a black poet born in Toledo, Ohio, attended the University of Toledo and is presently Writer-in-Residence at Indiana University and Purdue University. Her poems have been collected in various anthologies and her style is marked by its ironic tone, its short line length, and its verse techniques which indicate the influence of twentieth-century American writers such as e. e. cummings.

FERLINGHETTI, LAWRENCE (b. 1919), was born in New York and received his M.A. from Columbia University. In addition to writing he maintains a publishing house in San Francisco noted for publishing Allen Ginsberg's *Howl.* He has been influential among a group of poets known as the "Beats," whose poetry is characterized by social protest.

FROST, ROBERT (1874–1963), is usually associated with rural New England, where he spent most of his life. He attended Dartmouth and Harvard for short periods and then tried teaching, farming, journalism, and shoemaking. After his return from England, where he lived for three years and first received critical acclaim, he began his numerous public readings and lectures. Frost served as a professor at many universities, and received honorary degrees from more than thirty colleges and universities. His lyrics, and descriptive, and narrative poems are well loved for their precise imagery of natural objects and rural characters, for their strong dramatic element, and for their implied attitude of devout reverence and belief. He was awarded the Pulitzer Prize four times.

GARCIA LORCA, FEDERICO (1898–1936), was born in Andalusia and studied law and literature in Granada. The influences of folk speech and folk poetry are apparent in his verse, which is rich in metaphorical language—metaphors drawn from nature as experienced by the peasant. In 1929 he visited New York, where he was intrigued by life in Harlem. When he returned to Spain his attention turned to playwriting. He was murdered by Falangist supporters of Generalissimo Franco during the Spanish Civil War.

GILBERT, SIR WILLIAM SCHWENCK (1836–1911), is famous as the lyricist and librettist in the operetta-writing team of Gilbert and Sullivan. Born in England, he served in the militia, worked as a clerk in the Education Department, and then practiced law. His work is noted for its brilliant satirical wit directed at Victorian mores and often at his three earlier professions: the military, the civil service, and the law.

GINSBERG, ALLEN (b. 1926), was born in New Jersey and attended Columbia University. He was associated with the Beat movement in San Francisco and New York and lived in India for a while. His interest in Eastern philosophy has been taken up by many others, especially the young, for whom he has become a culture hero.

GIOVANNI, NIKKI (b. 1943), attended Fisk University and the University of Pennsylvania. She writes both prose and poetry.

GRAVES, ROBERT (b. 1895), English poet, critic, and novelist was the son of a gifted Irish poet, Alfred Perceval Graves. He enlisted in the Royal Welsh Fusiliers in World War I, after which he attended Oxford (he was later named Professor of Poetry there). He has spent most of his time since 1929 in Majorca. He has a rich background in classical studies, which is reflected in his poems and novels.

GRAY, THOMAS (1716–1771), was born in London and studied at Cambridge, where he later became Professor of History and Modern Languages. He was offered the poet laureateship but refused it. His poetry, maintaining classic form, anticipated the new nineteenth-century romanticism in its interests.

GUEVARA, MIGUEL DE (1585?–1646?), was an Augustin monk from the province of Michoacan in Mexico who traveled among the Aztecs and other tribes as a missionary. He directed many priories and was one of the foremost poets of his day.

HARDY, THOMAS (1840–1928), English novelist and poet, was born into a builder's family in Dorsetshire, the Wessex of his novels. He was first apprenticed to an architect but gave that up when he had achieved success as a novelist. When his last novel, *Jude the Obscure*, outraged Victorian critics, Hardy returned to his first love, poetry, producing nearly a thousand poems in the last thirty years of his life.

HAYDEN, ROBERT (b. 1913), was born in Detroit, Michigan, receiving his B.A. at Wayne State University and his M.A. at the University of Michigan, where he taught English for several years. He then joined the faculty of Fisk University and is now Professor of English there. He has been awarded a Rosenwald Fellowship and a Ford Foundation grant. In 1965, he received the Grand Prize for Poetry at the First World Festival of Negro Arts held in Dakar, Senegal.

HERBERT, GEORGE (1593–1633), English clergyman and poet, was the son of Lady Magdalen Herbert, to whom John Donne addressed his Holy Sonnets. He received his M.A. from Trinity College, Cambridge, and distinguished himself as a Latin and Greek scholar. After his ordination in the Anglican Church, he became an impassioned orator and preacher, and his verse is concerned with the communing of a soul with God.

HERRICK, ROBERT (1591–1674), English poet, was the son of a London goldsmith. He received his M.A. from St. John's in Cambridge and spent several years afterward in the company of Ben Jonson and his circle until he became a vicar in Devonshire. He is considered the most pagan of English poets; youth, love, and the pagan fields were his most prominent themes.

HOOD, THOMAS (1799–1845), English poet and humorist, was born in London, the son of a Scottish bookseller. At 16 he began writing for local newspapers and magazines. After a brief apprenticeship to his uncle, an engraver, he became the editor of several periodicals in which he published many of his own poems.

HOPKINS, GERARD MANLEY (1844–1889), born to an Anglican family, studied at Oxford, where he met Robert Bridges and was converted to Catholicism. He also studied in a Jesuit school under Cardinal Newman. When he converted, he destroyed his early attempts at poetry, but after a tragedy in which five nuns drowned, he commemorated their deaths in a poem and continued to write seriously. His verse was published only in 1918 and found a belatedly appreciative audience. He possessed one of the finest ears of any recent poet for extremely sensitive alliteration, assonance, and dissonance, and his innovations in language and rhythm have much influenced twentieth-century poetry.

HOUSMAN, ALFRED EDWARD (1859–1936), English poet and a distinguished scholar, was Professor of Latin at University College, London, and was later elected to the Kennedy Chair of Latin at Cambridge. He has achieved a great reputation from a very small body of work—twenty-five years elapsed between his first and second books—and his highly compressed style is probably due to the discipline of classical scholarship and the terseness of the Latin language. His poems revolve around his central themes of the passing of spring and youth and the brevity and tragedy of life.

HUGHES, LANGSTON (1902–1967), was born in Joplin, Missouri, the grandson of a participant in John Brown's raid at Harpers Ferry. During his youth he had many jobs, including that of a cabin boy on a freighter. Hughes was graduated from Lincoln University in Nebraska and attended Columbia. Hughes often used dialect and jazz rhythms in describing black life in his poetry. He also wrote novels, short stories, biographies, children's books, translations, and opera librettos.

ICAZA, FRANCISCO A. DE (1863–1925), critic, poet, and scholar, was born in Mexico but spent most of his years in Madrid. Icaza helped bring the work of many modern Mexican poets to public attention.

IGNATOW, DAVID (b. 1914), was born and educated in Brooklyn. He served as the editor of various magazines, was a Guggenheim Fellow, and has been poet-in-residence at York College and visiting lecturer at a number of universities.

ISAIAH, the first in order of the major Old Testament prophets, son of Amos, was a citizen of Jerusalem. He began to prophesy about the year 747 B.C. and exercised his office until the close of the century. The authenticity of the book of Isaiah has been doubted, but it is quite possible that the disputed prophecies do contain fragments from Isaiah himself.

JARRELL, RANDALL (1914–1965), was born in Nashville, Tennessee, grew up in California, and received his B.A. and M.A. from Vanderbilt University. American poet, teacher, and critic, was associated with the Southern literary group.

JEFFERS, JOHN ROBINSON (1887–1962), poet and playwright, was born in Pittsburgh. As a child he traveled through Europe and later studied at Occidental College. Jeffers finally settled in the Carmel–Big Sur area of California, the setting for much of his poetry. His narrative poems are filled with violence and horror, but his contribution to poetry lies mainly in the cut-from-stone elegance of his lyrics, revealing the beauty of permanence in rocks, sea, and sky.

JOHNSON, JAMES WELDON (1871–1938), poet and novelist, was born in Florida, where he was the first black admitted to the bar. He was educated at Atlanta University and at Columbia. At various times he was a teacher, school principal, Broadway lyricist, lawyer, United States Consul to Venezuela and Nicaragua, executive secretary of the NAACP, and Professor of Creative Literature at Fisk University. He had a great appreciation of the slave spirituals and frequently made use of the cadence and rhetoric of Negro sermons in his poems.

JONES, LEROI (b. 1934), poet and playwright, was born in New Jersey and graduated from Howard University. He attended Columbia and the New School for Social Research, served in the Air Force, and has been a Whitney and Guggenheim Fellow. Jones is a militant spokesman for black nationalism.

JONSON, BEN (1572–1637), renowned English poet and playwright, was also a bricklayer, soldier, and traveling actor. He killed a fellow actor in a duel, became a Catholic while in prison (but later recanted), and saved himself by pleading benefit of clergy. He was a contemporary of Shakespeare's and many consider that his lyric genius was second only to the Bard's. In his long career as writer of court masques during the reigns of Elizabeth I and James I, he was Poet Laureate, in fact if not in name.

KEATS, JOHN (1795–1821), the son of a livery-stable keeper in London, was first apprenticed to a surgeon. Keats died of tuberculosis at the age of 26. Today he is considered one of the finest poets to have written in the English language, but ironically his first volume of poems was considered too "Cockney" by his contemporaries. He delighted in the world of the eye, ear, and touch, and made a constant effort to make the senses talk—for him, the imagination was the supreme gift.

KIPLING, RUDYARD (1865–1936), the son of an English architectural sculptor, was born in Bombay, India, and educated in England. He returned to India at the age of 17 as a journalist. Kipling is known for a large body of work including poems, novels, short stories, newspaper articles, and children's literature. He was the recipient of many honors, and in 1907 became the first Englishman to receive the Nobel Prize for Literature. He became identified with the spirit of nationalism and imperialism, and was tremendously popular during his lifetime. Kipling is less popular now, but critics such as T. S. Eliot have found much of value in his work.

LANDOR, WALTER SAVAGE (1775–1864), English poet and essayist, inherited a fortune from his father, much of which he later squandered. His domestic life and his career were stormy. Although there has been a recent revival of interest in his poetry, Landor remains one of the great eccentrics in English literature.

LAWRENCE, DAVID HERBERT (1885–1930), the son of a Nottingham miner, worked first as a school teacher after graduating from the University College in Nottingham, then dedicated his life to being a poet, novelist, short story writer, essayist, and playwright. In 1912 he eloped with a married woman whom he later married; subsequently he and his wife, Frieda Lawrence, lived in Italy, England, Australia, and New Mexico. He is most famous for his novels, which often dealt with the themes of sexuality, and was prosecuted for obscenity several times. He also explored the subconscious forces in men's lives and believed in the necessity for following instinctual feelings rather than sterile, cerebral consciousness.

LEVERTOV, DENISE (b. 1923), was born in England, where she studied mainly with tutors. She came to the United States in 1948 and became a citizen in 1955. She has written poetry from an early age and has been on the faculty of many colleges and the recipient of many poetry awards.

LINDSAY, NICHOLAS VACHEL (1879–1931), was born in Springfield, Ohio. He studied art, but earned his living "on the road," often giving verses in exchange for lodging and food. Never shy, and often eccentric, he often gave oral readings of his own poetry.

LONGFELLOW, HENRY WADSWORTH (1807–1882), descendant of an old colonial family, was born in Portland, Maine. He graduated from Bowdoin College in the same year as Nathaniel Hawthorne. He studied abroad and returned to teach at Bowdoin and later at Harvard. Longfellow was enormously popular during his lifetime because of his gift for simple, romantic story-telling in verse and his ability to understand and express the aspirations and sorrows of every day life.

LORCA. See GARCIA LORCA, FEDERICO.

LOVELACE, RICHARD (1618–1658), an English Cavalier poet, was born to and enjoyed the courtly life that is reflected in his verse. He spent his fortune for the royalist cause, and when the Puritans came to power, he suffered for it, dying in extreme want. Apart from a few excellent lyrics, his poetry is considered extravagant, rhetorical, and artificial.

LOWELL, AMY (1874–1925), belonged to a family noted for its prominence in education and letters in New England's history. She was a key figure in the imagist group of poets that also included Robert Frost and Carl Sandburg.

LOWELL, ROBERT (b. 1917), was born in Boston of a distinguished literary family that included the poet Amy Lowell. He studied at Harvard and at Kenyon College, where he was graduated *summa cum laude*. His conversion to Catholicism combined with his strong Puritan heritage have contributed to the rich symbolism of his poetry. He has been awarded the Pulitzer Prize, a Guggenheim Fellowship, and served as Consultant in Poetry to the Library of Congress.

LYLY, JOHN (1554–1606), English poet, dramatist, prose writer, and member of Parliament, is most famous for the ornate, affected style of writing that was called euphuism after his novel, *Euphues*. This style consisted of the frequent use of antithesis, alliteration, and allusion. He was a contemporary of Sidney and Spenser and had an influence on Jonson and Shakespeare, for he showed the importance of prose as an art form and he made literature of plays.

MCGINLEY, PHYLLIS (b. 1905), was born in Oregon and studied at a number of colleges, including the University of Utah and Columbia. Her light verse is largely based on her observations and experiences as a suburban wife and mother. In 1961 she was awarded the Pulitzer Prize for poetry.

MCKAY, CLAUDE (1891–1948), a prominent figure in the "Harlem Renaissance" of the 1920s and the American radical press of post–World War I vintage, was born in Jamaica and immigrated to the United States in 1912. He attended Kansas State University, then came to New York City, devoting the rest of his life to literary and editorial activities. After having worked as associate editor of *The Liberator*, he visited the Soviet Union for six months. He then lived in Europe for ten years, often in contact with the prominent American expatriate writers of the 1920s. His first novel, *Home to Harlem*, was a bestseller and won the Harmon Gold Award for Literature.

MACLEISH, ARCHIBALD (b. 1892), was born in Illinois, graduated from Yale, received a law degree from Harvard, and served in World War I. He served as Librarian of Congress and as Assistant Secretary of State under Franklin Roosevelt, and helped to organize UNESCO. He is known for his radio and verse plays as well as for his poems and essays, and has three times been awarded the Pulitzer Prize.

MACNEICE, LOUIS (1907–1963), was born in Belfast, Ireland, the son of an Anglican bishop. During the 1930s he was associated with Auden and Spender as a poet of social protest. He wrote radio scripts for the BBC in addition to his poetry and also produced several volumes of literary criticism.

MARLOWE, CHRISTOPHER (1564–1593), Elizabethan poet and dramatist, was the son of a shoemaker. Educated at Cambridge, he soon left it for London, where he devoted himself to the theater and to politics. Earlier dramatists had employed blank verse, but it had been stiff and ungainly. Marlowe was the first to discover its strength and variety, thereby much influencing the works of Shakespeare and Milton. A brawl in a tavern, probably connected with political intrigue, ended his short but brilliant career.

MARTINEZ, ENRIQUE GONZALEZ (1871–1952), was one of the recluses of Mexican literature. Nevertheless, he published a great list of works spanning over forty years.

MARVELL, ANDREW (1621–1678), English metaphysical poet, satirist, and pamphleteer, was the son of an Anglican clergyman. He first served as a tutor (at which time he wrote most of his poetry) and later entered politics as a member of Parliament. During his life he was known for his satire; most of his poems were published posthumously.

MASTERS, EDGAR LEE (1869–1950), was born in Kansas, grew up in Illinois, and worked as a lawyer in Chicago. Writing was at first only a hobby with him. *The Spoon River Anthology*, his most famous work, is a collection of portraits, often sardonic, of men and women living in a small Midwestern town.

MATTHEW (1st century), one of the Twelve Apostles, was a tax gatherer before becoming a disciple of Jesus. According to tradition, he was the author of the first gospel of the New Testament, was a missionary to the Hebrews, and suffered martyrdom.

MEREDITH, GEORGE (1828–1909), English poet and novelist, was born at Portsmouth, the grandson of a famous tailor, and educated privately in Germany. His chief poetic work is the autobiographical sonnet sequence, *Modern Love,* which deals with incompatibility of temper. His two master themes were the "reading of earth" and the sex duel. As a publisher's reader he encouraged Thomas Hardy and George Gissing and at his death he was a dominant force in British letters.

MEREDITH, WILLIAM (b. 1919), graduated *magna cum laude* from Princeton, worked as copyboy and reporter on *The New York Times,* and served in the air force in World War II. He has taught at Princeton and at Connecticut College.

MILLAY, EDNA ST. VINCENT (1892–1950), was born in Maine and was graduated from Vassar College. She won early fame with her poem, "Renascence," a remarkable achievement for a girl of 19. Her work, in addition to poetry, includes verse dramas and an operatic libretto. She was the first woman to be awarded the Pulitzer Prize for poetry.

MILTON, JOHN (1608–1674), English poet and pamphleteer, was the son of a scrivener and composer of music. England was torn by conflict in which religion was a violently political issue, and Milton, though fiercely independent in his religious thinking, served as Latin Secretary to the Puritan leader, Oliver Cromwell. Partially from overwork, he became blind at the age of 43. When the royalist government was reinstated he retired from politics, free at last to compose the religious epic for which he is' most famous, *Paradise Lost.*

MOORE, MARIANNE (1887–1972), was born in St. Louis and graduated from Bryn Mawr. She has lived mainly in New York City and combines great knowledge with a strong love of baseball. In 1951 she was awarded the Pulitzer Prize.

NASH, OGDEN (1902–1971), author of light verse famous for unusual rhymes, he worked for a publisher in New York. His quick wit made him a popular television panelist.

NEMEROV, HOWARD (b. 1920), graduated from Harvard and served as a pilot in World War II. He teaches English at Brandeis University, and writes both fiction and verse.

OWEN, WILFORD (1893–1918), an English poet, served in World War I. He was killed in action on the Western Front shortly before the armistice, and his antiwar verse was published posthumously by his friend, the poet Siegfried Sassoon. His poems were distinguished by the use of assonance in place of rhyme.

PAUL (1st century), the Apostle to the Gentiles, was born of Jewish parents at Tarsus in Celicia. Trained as a rabbi, he was a strenuous Pharisee and assisted in persecuting the Christians until a vision of the Crucifixion converted him into a fervent adherent of the new faith. He is the author of the Epistles to the Galatians, Romans, and Corinthians (1st and 2nd).

PAZ, OCTAVIO (b. 1914), poet, essayist, and anthologist, was born in Mexico City, studied at the university there, and went to Spain during the Civil War. He is the recipient of many awards including a Guggenheim Fellowship in 1944. He has held diplomatic posts in Japan, France, and India.

PLATH, SYLVIA (1932–1963), American poet born in Massachusetts, was graduated from Smith College, where she later taught, and studied for a time at Cambridge University. She published her well-received volume of poems, *The Colossus,* in 1960, in England, where she lived with her husband Ted Hughes, an English poet, until her suicide at the age of 31.

POE, EDGAR ALLAN (1809–1849), was born in Boston, the son of actors who died when he was very young. He was raised by a tobacco exporter, John Allan of Virginia, who sent him to the University of Virginia and West Point, but they quarreled and Poe left school. He married his 13-year-old cousin, Virginia Clemm, who died early of tuberculosis. Poe wrote poems, stories, and criticism, and worked as a magazine editor. His poems were a major influence on the French symbolists, Baudelaire and Mallarmé, and his literary criticism greatly influenced modern theories of literature.

POPE, ALEXANDER (1688–1744), English poet and satirist, was the son of a linen draper. He became enormously erudite through self-education despite two strikes against him in his youth: as the son of Catholics, he was virtually ostracized; and a serious illness left him a four-foot-six-inch hunchback. Nevertheless, he made a fortune from his translations of the classics, and became the leading literary figure in England. With Pope, the heroic couplet became so important a poetic form that it dominated English verse until the romantic poets rebelled against its use.

POUND, EZRA LOOMIS (1885–1972), born in Idaho, attended the University of Pennsylvania and Hamilton College, where he was awarded a Ph.D. at the age of 20. After a brief stint at teaching, he went to live in Europe, where he became literary mentor for such writers as Yeats and Eliot, and leader of the expatriate "Lost Generation" in the 1920s. During World War II he broadcast Fascist radio propaganda, and after the war he was to be tried for treason but was adjudged insane, and committed to a Washington, D.C., sanitarium. On his release he returned to Italy. Opinion about his poetry is mixed, but there is no question of his influence on other major poets.

RANSOM, JOHN CROWE (b. 1888), poet, educator, and critic, was born in Tennessee. He was a Rhodes Scholar at Oxford and later taught at Vanderbilt University and at Kenyon College, where he founded and has since been editor of the *Kenyon Review*. His influence has been felt, not in literary circles alone, but in the academic world as well.

ROETHKE, THEODORE (1908–1963), was born in Michigan and graduated from its state university. He studied at Harvard and taught at various universities. He was awarded the Pulitzer Prize in 1953 and the Bollingen Prize in 1958 for collections of his early and late works of poetry. These poems show great variety and sensitivity and many include the plant imagery of growth and decay that prevades so much of his work.

ROSSETTI, CHRISTINA GEORGINA (1830–1894), English poet, wrote lyric poems and verse for children as well as religious prose. She was devoutly religious and for the last years of her life lived at home as a recluse and invalid. She was the sister of Dante Gabriel Rossetti, the poet.

ROSSETTI, DANTE GABRIEL (1828–1882), was the son of an Italian political refugee and was educated at King's College, London. He studied painting and was prominent in the PreRaphaelite Brotherhood, a group of artists who tried to recapture in their work the qualities of Italian religious art before Raphael. As a poet, he is known for his sonnets and ballads; he is also remembered for his translation of Dante.

RUKEYSER, MURIEL (b. 1913), was born in New York City and attended Vassar College. She is the author of poems, biographies, motion picture and television scripts. She was on the faculty of Sarah Lawrence College for many years and is the recipient of several awards, including a Guggenheim Fellowship in 1943.

SANDBURG, CARL AUGUST (1878–1967), poet and biographer, was born in Illinois to a Swedish immigrant family. His schooling was sporadic and at 13 he began the long series of odd jobs that included hoboing. In Wisconsin he was an organizer for the Socialist-Democrat party and secretary to the mayor of Milwaukee. Then he moved to Chicago and became a newspaper man. His poems and biographies reveal his consuming interest in America, and his famous Lincoln biography brought him the 1940 Pulitzer Prize.

SASSOON, SIEGFRIED (1886–1967), an English poet, studied two years at Cambridge. When World War I broke out, he enlisted and served, and this experience provided him (as it had Wilfred Owen) with the material for much angry antiwar poetry, testifying bitterly to the ingloriousness of modern warfare. However, he later disowned pacifism. In 1951 was designated a Commander of the British Empire. In 1957 he became a Roman Catholic.

SCHWARTZ, DELMORE (1913–1966), was born in Brooklyn and graduated from New York University. He was a poet, critic, and teacher, and an editor of the *Partisan Review*.

SCOTT, SIR WALTER (1771–1832), Scottish historical novelist, scholar, and poet, was born in Edinburgh, attended its university, and studied law in his father's office. During his life he fought with courage, first against the crippling effects of infantile paralysis, which left him lame, and later to pay off the debts of his nearly bankrupt publishing house. Scott's most illustrious career was that of historical novelist, as evidenced by the Waverly novels, which include his classics *The Bride of Lammermoor* and *Ivanhoe*.

SHAKESPEARE, WILLIAM (1564–1616), the greatest English dramatist and poet, was born at Stratford-upon-Avon. Few facts of his life are known except that he married at 18 and may have taught school for a while. In London he worked as actor, playwright, and producer. His literary output was enormous: poems, sonnets, and approximately two plays a year over a fifteen-year period. He acquired a modest fortune and was able to retire comfortably to Stratford in 1613. He has been considered the greatest interpreter of human relationships and the supreme observer of human frailties and potentialities.

SHAPIRO, KARL (b. 1913), was born in Baltimore but has lived mostly in Nebraska, where he taught at the state university. He studied law at the University of Virginia and Johns Hopkins, and during World War II he served in the South Pacific. He was awarded the Pulitzer Prize for poetry in 1945 and is now Professor of English at the University of California at Davis.

SHELLEY, PERCY BYSSHE (1792–1822), was born in Sussex and educated at Eton and Oxford, from which he and another student were expelled for publishing their pamphlet "The Necessity of Atheism." His second wife was Mary Wollstonecraft Godwin, the author of *Frankenstein*. They lived mainly in Italy, where they spent much time with the poet Byron and where Shelley wrote much of his finest poetry. His lyricism, effortless as breathing, pervades all of his poetry. When only 30 he drowned while sailing.

SHIRLEY, JAMES (1596–1666), was born in London and educated at Oxford and Cambridge. He left schoolteaching when he converted to Catholicism and began to write plays. During his lifetime, he produced over forty dramatic works. Severely burned in the Great Fire of London, he and his wife died the next day.

SIDNEY, SIR PHILIP (1554–1586), came from a noble English family but for most of his life was poor. He studied at Oxford and Cambridge and traveled extensively throughout Europe. He was widely celebrated in his life time as a courtier and literary figure (though nothing was published until after his death) and even more so as a man of affairs in the court of Elizabeth I. He died after receiving a fatal wound in the war against Spain.

SIMON, PAUL (b. 1941), was born in Forest Hills, New York, near his future partner Art Garfunkel. They attended the same public school and became friends there. Paul Simon went to Queens College and Brooklyn Law School, and then to England to perform as an American folksinger. He was joined there by Garfunkel, and their meteoric rise to fame began. Known as "a poet and a one man band," the team, besides recording many albums, also wrote the score for the movie *The Graduate*.

SIMPSON, LOUIS (b. 1923), an American poet born in the British West Indies, attended Columbia University, where he received a Ph.D. He served in the air force in World War II, was on the faculty of the University of California, Berkeley, and is now at the State University of New York, Stony Brook. He was awarded the Pulitzer Prize for poetry in 1964.

SOLOMON (c. 1015–977 B.C.), king of Israel, was the second son of David and Bathsheba. His reign was outwardly splendid and he was credited with transcendent wisdom. However, it is now doubted whether he ever authored the works to which his name has been attached—Proverbs, Ecclesiastes, the Song of Solomon, and the Wisdom of Solomon.

SOUTHEY, ROBERT (1774–1843), English poet, biographer, and historian, son of a Bristol linen draper, was expelled from the Westminster School for his essay against flogging. He went to Oxford, where Coleridge converted him to Unitarianism and Pantisocracy; they planned to develop a utopian community but failed to raise funds for it. He settled with his family at Keswick, sharing a double house with the Coleridges. For the last thirty years of his life he held the post of England's Poet Laureate.

SPENDER, STEPHEN (b. 1909), English poet, translator, editor, and critic, was the son of a prominent liberal journalist. Educated at Oxford, he was in the 1930s one of the "modern poets" and associated with the circle of young poets that included Auden, MacNeice, and C. Day Lewis. He served in the Spanish Civil War and as a fireman during World War II. He has lectured widely and has taught at a number of American universities.

SPENSER, EDMUND (1552–1599), born in London, son of a gentleman tradesman, received his M.A. degree from Cambridge. In his day England's foremost poet, his popularity is due largely to The Faerie Queen, his long allegorical poem honoring Queen Elizabeth, which was designed to show the ideal gentleman or courtier in action—a favorite Renaissance theme.

SPINDEN, HERBERT JOSEPH (1879–1967), was born in Huron, South Dakota, and received his Ph.D. at Harvard. He worked as an anthropologist and archeologist and became curator of Indian art and primitive cultures at the Brooklyn Museum. An authority on ancient art and ancient American history, he worked out the chronology of Mayan inscriptions and the Mayan civil and Venus calendars.

STEVENS, WALLACE (1879–1955), was born in Pennsylvania and educated at Harvard College and New York University Law School. He practiced law and did well in business, becoming vice-president of a Hartford insurance company. Much of his poetry was written after his fortieth year and it is said that he frequently jotted it on slips of paper while he was going to work.

However poetry was no mere hobby; he won the Pulitzer Prize in 1955 and is among the finest modern poets.

SUCKLING, SIR JOHN (1609–1642), inherited a large estate in England, made the grand tour of Europe, and returned to England to be knighted and live in elegant style. He wrote both plays and poems, and was enormously popular for his quick wit and courtly ways. He enjoyed cards and invented the game of cribbage. When Charles I was defeated, Suckling is said to have committed suicide, unable to face the certain loss of his fortune.

SURREY, HENRY HOWARD (1517?–1547), was named an English earl by courtesy. With his friend Thomas Wyatt he popularized the sonnet and introduced the use of blank verse. He served during the war in France, was accused of a trivial crime, and beheaded.

SWIFT, JONATHAN (1667–1745), was born in Dublin, the son of especially *Gulliver's Travels,* and stands as one of the great satirists of all time. A man of contradictory impulses, he was made Dean of St. Patrick's Cathedral, in Dublin—a dubious honor at the time since it represented exile from London. He reportedly died insane.

SWINBURNE, ALGERNON CHARLES (1837–1909), English poet, critic and dramatist, was descended from nobility. Wordsworth stimulated his interest in poetry and he eventually joined the Pre-Raphaelite group that included Dante Rossetti. He rebelled against restraint, of the senses or in politics, which resulted in his theme of the assertion of man's dignity. His works represent the last phase of the romantic movement.

TABLADA, JOSE JUAN (1871–1945), poet, art critic, and journalist, he introduced *haiku* into the Spanish language.

TENNYSON, ALFRED, LORD (1809–1892), was the son of a rector. He attended Trinity College, Cambridge, where he was awarded a medal for poetry. He was enormously popular with his contemporaries and he succeeded Wordsworth as England's Poet Laureate. The peerage was bestowed on him in 1883, paying tribute to him as Lord Tennyson, the perfect mirror of the Victorian era. He is best known today for *In Memoriam* and *Idylls of the King,* which he based on the Arthurian legends.

THOMAS, DYLAN MARLAIS (1914–1953), was born in Swansea, Wales, and lived in London through World War II. His rich poetic style, with its vivid though often obscure imagery, had a great effect upon his generation. Through his lecture tours and readings he achieved great personal popularity, and he may yet well be

judged the greatest lyric poet of his generation and a fiction writer
of original humor and charm. His early death in New York City
resulted from acute alcoholism.

UPDIKE, JOHN (b. 1932), American novelist and poet, was born
in Pennsylvania, the scene of much of his work. He graduated
summa cum laude from Harvard, and for a time worked for *The
New Yorker* magazine. His novel *The Centaur* received the Na-
tional Book Award.

WALKER, MARGARET ABIGAIL (b. 1915), was born in Birmingham,
Alabama, the daughter of a Methodist minister. She was grad-
uated from Northwestern University and received a Ph.D. from
Iowa State University. She has taught English at several colleges,
and has worked as a social worker and a reporter.

WHITMAN, WALT (1819–1892), was born on Long Island and
later moved to Brooklyn, where he worked as a teacher, a printer,
and a newspaper editor. He read widely and received little formal
education. When his volume of poems *Leaves Of Grass* was pub-
lished in 1855, it was generally ignored or considered unpoetic
(as free verse it didn't rhyme or have regular meter) and even
improper because of the frank language. Today it is an acknowl-
edged masterpiece in world literature.

WHITTIER, JOHN GREENLEAF (1807–1892), American poet and ab-
olitionist, was born in Massachusetts, the son of a poor farmer.
He is linked with the New England group of poets and in his day
was considered second only to Longfellow. His early poems ap-
peared chiefly in local newspapers and when he was 21 he em-
barked on a career of itinerant journalism. In 1833 he attended
an anti-slavery convention and for the next thirty years was a
zealous abolitionist. As the poet of rural New England and as a
voice of calm and sincere religious faith, he was enormously
popular and widely celebrated during his life.

WILBUR, RICHARD (b. 1921), studied at Amherst and Harvard and
taught at Harvard, Wellesley, and Wesleyan. He was influenced
by the French symbolists, and his excellent translations of
Moliere's plays have been performed on Broadway. He also co-
authored the lyrics for a musical comedy based on Voltaire's
Candide. He's received inumerable awards, including the Pulitzer
Prize in 1957.

WILLIAMS, WILLIAM CARLOS (1883–1963), poet and novelist, was
born and lived most of his life in Rutherford, New Jersey, where
he was a practicing physician. His works concentrated on the
world he knew and lived in, which involved a life-long poetic

search for the universals of human existence among the minutiae of everyday urban life.

WORDSWORTH, WILLIAM (1770–1850), English poet, was the son of an attorney. He made a walking tour of France and the Alps during the French Revolution, and became a defender of Rousseau and republicanism. A great poetic spokesman for the common man, his work conveys feelings of humanitarianism, liberalism, and a thoroughly panthiestic worship of nature. In the Lake Country, where he lived with his sister Dorothy, he met Coleridge and together they published *Lyrical Ballads,* an historic literary document which launched the romantic movement. Near the end of his long life Wordsworth was appointed Poet Laureate and became religiously and politically conservative.

WYLIE, ELINOR (1885–1928), poet and novelist, was born in New Jersey. Her parents were both descended from old Pennsylvania families distinguished in society and public affairs, and she attended private schools in Bryn Mawr and Washington. She caused quite a scandal when she eloped with a cultivated scholarly man, abandoning her first husband (who later committed suicide) and small son. In a space of just eight years she wrote four books of poems and four novels, in which her tragic vision of life is grained with fantasy and satire.

YEATS, WILLIAM BUTLER (1865–1939), Irish poet and dramatist, was the eldest son of a well-known Dublin painter. His long literary career spanned the Victorian and Edwardian periods and ended at the outbreak of World War II. He was interested in the occult and in mysticism and was an ardent nationalist; he helped found the Irish National Theatre Society, later to be the Abbey Theatre of Dublin. In 1923 he was awarded the Nobel Prize in Literature. Throughout his career he sought a philosophical and artistic system that would resolve the conflict between his vision of what art should be and the recognition of what life is.

Index of Authors

Index of Titles

327

Index of First Lines